The Science and Superpowers of Seaweed

Chris Adair

THE

Science

AND

Superpowers

OF

Seaweed

A GUIDE FOR KIDS

Amanda Swinimer

**HARBOUR
PUBLISHING**

For Mahina & Nesika,
my two biggest loves.

Harbour Publishing Co. Ltd.
P.O. Box 219, Madeira Park, BC, VON 2H0
www.harbourpublishing.com

All photographs by Amanda Swinimer except where otherwise noted.
Edited by Sarah Harvey
Indexed by Emma Biron
Cover and text design by Libris Simas Ferraz / Onça Publishing
Icons by Mitja Kurbos
Illustrations by Claire Watson
Back cover illustration by Claire Watson

Front cover photos:
top left by Nicole Yamamoto;
top right by Jeremy Koreski;
lower left by Eiko Jones;
lower right by Amanda Swinimer
Printed with vegetable-based ink on paper certified by the Forest Stewardship Council®
Printed and bound in South Korea

Harbour Publishing acknowledges the support of the Canada Council for the Arts, the Government of Canada, and the Province of British Columbia through the BC Arts Council.

Library and Archives Canada Cataloguing in Publication
Title: The science and superpowers of seaweed : a guide for kids / Amanda Swinimer.
Names: Swinimer, Amanda, author.
Description: Includes bibliographical references and index.
Identifiers: Canadiana (print) 20220480621 | Canadiana (ebook) 20220480672 | ISBN 9781990776199 (softcover) | ISBN 9781990776205 (EPUB)
Subjects: LCSH: Marine algae—Juvenile literature. | LCSH: Marine algae culture—Juvenile literature. | LCSH: Marine ecology—Juvenile literature. | LCSH: Kelp bed ecology—Juvenile literature.
Classification: LCC QK570.2 .S95 2023 | DDC j579.8/8—dc23

Contents

Jennifer Jellett

Introduction

Welcome to the watery and wonderful world of seaweed. I have always loved the ocean, and many years ago I harvested my first pieces of edible seaweed from the beach in front of my home on the west coast of Vancouver Island in British Columbia, Canada. I loved it so much that I became a professional seaweed harvester (yes, there is such a thing!). I spend so much time in the ocean that some people think I am a real-life mermaid, and I am often called the Mermaid of the Pacific. I love being in the ocean more than anywhere else.

I harvest seaweed in the **Salish Sea**, a distinct part of the Pacific Ocean that cradles the southern tip of Vancouver Island. The Salish Sea is the traditional territory of the Coast Salish peoples, who have lived here for at least ten thousand years!

One of the seaweeds I harvest is called bull kelp. Bull kelp is the second-largest seaweed on the planet and one of the fastest-growing organisms in the world. It can grow longer than forty metres, which is longer than a blue whale, the largest animal to ever live on Earth! Bull kelp is one kind of seaweed that forms underwater forests called **kelp forests**.

The kelp forests in the **Pacific Northwest** are made of seaweeds that are as tall as trees. The water in a kelp forest is the

An Ode to Seaweed

Each time I dive into the sea
I feel a sense of mystery.

Seaweed shimmering in the sun
Shore crabs doing their sideways run.

Kelp fronds follow the current's flow,
Tall as trees in the turquoise glow.

So many sizes, shapes and shades
Of seaweeds, dancing in the waves.

Dulse and nori, kombu, bull kelp,
Mineral-rich to heal and help.

They nourish land and air and sea
And I thank them for nourishing me.

1

That little black dot in the centre of the photograph is me! I am harvesting a seaweed called bull kelp. *Jennifer Jellett*

This is what it looks like underneath the surface. Here I am swimming in a bull kelp forest. *Chris Adair*

Rainbow seaweed underwater on a sunny day.

Do you know what a **phycologist** is? Most people do not! Even your teacher or your parents may not know. But I can tell you: a phycologist is a scientist who studies seaweed. The science of seaweed is called **phycology**. Throughout the book I will share with you cool phyco-facts about seaweed.

colour of shimmering emeralds. Many fascinating sea creatures live in the kelp forest, such as crabs, jellyfish, seals, sea lions and sometimes even orcas, grey whales and humpback whales. And fish: *lots* of fish. Sometimes there are so many fish that all you can see in every direction are fish weaving in and out of giant seaweeds. As a professional seaweed harvester, the kelp forest is where I work. It is my "office."

Seaweeds are my passion: they always amaze me, and I am constantly learning new things about them. They are beautiful, mysterious and enchanting. Some seaweeds are among the most ancient life forms on Earth. There are seaweeds that are so tiny it is hard to even see them unless there are a lot growing together, and some seaweeds are the length of three school buses! Seaweeds can be many different colours—pink, purple, golden yellow, emerald

Introduction   **3**

green—and some are iridescent, shimmering all the colours of the rainbow like a treasure trove of jewels. Seaweeds can also be many different shapes. For example, there is a seaweed that is shaped like a little palm tree, some are covered in tiny holes, some are squishy like a sponge and one looks like a big bull whip.

Seaweeds have been used as medicines for thousands of years, and recently scientists are discovering many substances found only in seaweed that can help to protect against disease. Seaweeds are also full of healthy **vitamins** and have more **minerals** than any other food!

Seaweeds are also critical to the health of the planet. For example, did you know that they produce oxygen that we need to breathe, help to keep the Earth cool and provide nourishment for thousands of kinds of sea creatures?

I am so excited to share all the amazing things I have learned about seaweeds, and to introduce you to some of the common seaweeds you can find on both the Pacific and Atlantic coasts of North America. I'll also tell you about some cool things you can do with seaweed. Are you ready to dive under the cold green water with me and learn all about the *amazing* and *awesome*, the *extraordinary* and *enchanting* world of seaweed?

Which Seaweeds Are Kelp?

When you see this icon beside a seaweed, you know it is a kelp. Remember, all kelp belong to the brown seaweed group.

My niece with a type of kelp called sieve kelp.

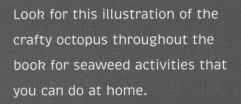

Look for this illustration of the crafty octopus throughout the book for seaweed activities that you can do at home.

These icons are used in the seaweed profiles throughout this book to indicate which oceans each seaweed can be found in:

 Atlantic Ocean

 Pacific Ocean

Arctic Ocean

Southern Ocean

What Is Seaweed?

Seaweeds are like the plants of the sea. Like plants on land, seaweeds need sunlight to grow, just like we need food to grow. When plants or seaweeds use sunlight to grow, we call this **photosynthesis**. Also, like plants, seaweeds are **sedentary**. This means they can't move around. You've never seen a tree walking around, have you? Well, seaweeds don't walk around either. Whereas a plant's roots anchor them to the ground, seaweeds anchor to rocks, sedentary animals like barnacles, and sometimes even other seaweeds with something called a **holdfast**. Seaweeds usually have a part that looks like a stem, which is called a **stipe**, and a part that looks like a leaf, which is called the **blade** or the **frond**.

Some of the ways seaweeds are similar to plants:

- Many seaweeds look like plants.
- Seaweeds photosynthesize like plants.
- Seaweeds and plants are sedentary (they can't move around).

Opposite: Low tide exposes so many beautiful seaweeds!

holdfast

stipe

blade or frond

Parts of a seaweed. This seaweed is five-rib kelp. *Emma Geiger*

Some of the ways seaweeds are different from plants:

- Seaweeds do not have roots.
- Seaweeds do not have flowers, fruits or cones.
- Plants absorb nutrients from the soil through their roots, and then those nutrients travel to other parts of the plants such as their leaves. Seaweeds absorb the nutrients they need directly from the seawater. The whole seaweed can absorb nutrients, whereas a plant can only absorb nutrients through its roots. Nutrients are substances that every living thing needs to grow and to stay alive. The food that you eat contains nutrients that *you* need to stay alive.

The Different Groups of Seaweeds

Seaweeds are divided into three main groups: brown sea-weeds, red seaweeds and green seaweeds. I like to think of these groups as being the three different seaweed families.

Bull kelp is a brown seaweed.

Dulse is a red seaweed.

Sea lettuce is a green seaweed.

Emma Geiger

Phyco-fact

Phycologists estimate there are at least 650 species of seaweed that grow in the Pacific Northwest, with new species still being discovered.

Are Kelp Seaweeds?

Yes! Kelp are a special group of closely-related seaweeds in the brown seaweed group and includes the largest seaweeds on Earth! While some types of kelp do not float but grow close to the ground, others grow upward toward the surface. These types of kelp form the structure of an ecosystem called a kelp forest. Kelp forest ecosystems are very **biodiverse** and are home to a tremendous amount of life. Kelp is very healthy for both people and the planet.

Are Seaweeds Algae?

Yes! All seaweeds are part of a larger group of organisms called **algae**. Large algae, like seaweeds, are called **macroalgae** (*macro* means big). There are many kinds of algae that are so small you can only see them with a microscope. These tiny algae are called **microalgae** (*micro* means small). Most microalgae are composed of just one cell and can live almost anywhere on Earth. They can live in every part of the ocean, including at the very bottom, which is eleven kilometres (almost seven miles) deep at the deepest part! They can live in lakes, ponds and rivers, and in the snow on the top of a mountain. They can even live *on* animals such as turtles, sloths, salamanders and polar bears! Both macroalgae and microalgae photosynthesize, which means they use the energy from the sun to grow, and they produce **oxygen**, which we need to breathe.

Ancient Algae

Scientists believe that microalgae called cyanobacteria were one of the first living things on Earth. The earliest fossils of cyanobacteria are 3.5 billion years old!

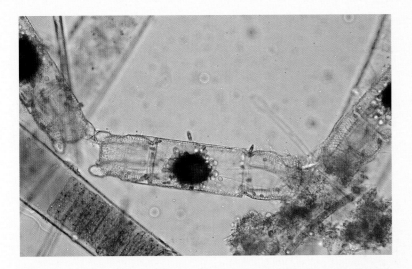

This is a picture of two types of microalgae. The lower left organism with purple is a cyanobacterium. The organisms that look like a clear chain with brown splotches in the centre are called **diatoms**. Diatoms have a glass-like component called silica in their cell walls that gives them very beautiful patterns. Diatoms and cyanobacteria are so small that you need a microscope to be able to see them.

Thomas Frankovich

Phyco-fact

Corals, which are tiny animals, need microalgae to survive. Microalgae called **zooxanthellae** provide nutrients to the coral, and the coral provides the microalgae with a place to live. Scientists call this type of close relationship a **symbiotic relationship**. The microalgae also give colour to the coral they live inside. Coral that doesn't have microalgae living inside it turns bright white. Scientists call this *coral bleaching*. Coral can't survive for very long without microalgae, as it needs the microalgae for food.

Why Is That Sloth Green?

Eyeworld

A type of microalga that grows on the fur of sloths gives their coat a green hue. When sloths groom themselves by licking their fur, they consume the algae. Scientists think the algae provide a significant part of sloths' nutrients, and that sloths may not be able to survive without them. This particular alga is not known to grow anywhere else in the world— only on sloth fur!

Where Do Seaweeds Grow?

Seaweeds grow in the ocean in the **intertidal zone** and **subtidal zone**. The intertidal zone is an area of the shore that is sometimes underwater and sometimes not, depending on whether the tide is high or low. There are three main areas of the intertidal zone: the **high intertidal zone**, the **mid-intertidal zone** and the **low intertidal zone**.

The high intertidal zone is the area of the intertidal zone that is the farthest away from the water's edge and is often exposed to air. Nori and sea lettuce can be found growing in the high intertidal zone.

The mid-intertidal zone is underwater about half the time, when the tide is coming in, and exposed to air about

half the time, when the tide is going out. Lots of seaweeds grow in the mid-intertidal zone. Here we can find seaweeds such as rockweed and Turkish washcloth.

The low intertidal zone is an area of the shore closest to the water's edge that is underwater most of the time. It is only exposed to air when the tide is very low. Winged kelp, feather boa and rainbow seaweed can be found in the low intertidal zone.

The subtidal zone is an area of the ocean that is always underwater, no matter how low the tide is. Seaweeds that grow in the subtidal zone include bull kelp, giant kelp and oarweed.

Seaweeds and the different areas of the tidal zone where they grow.

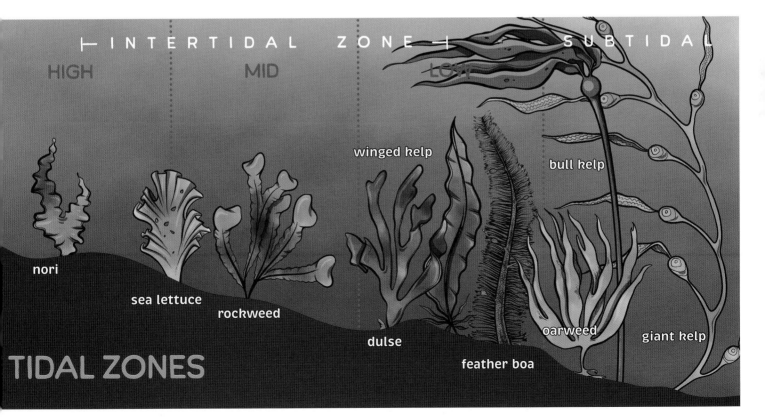

Octopus Oasis

One of my favourite things about being a seaweed harvester is that I get to have some incredible experiences with sea creatures while snorkelling and harvesting seaweed in a kelp forest. Once I peered through my mask and saw the head of a giant Pacific octopus just in front of me, nestled into the fronds of the bull kelp. It was huge: about the size of a pillow. When I finally managed to pull my gaze away from the octopus's head, I could see its arms, which looked like tentacles covered in suction cups, weaving in and out of the bull kelps for as far as I could see. I hung weightless in the water, staring at the octopus in complete fascination, for a long time.

At the time, I knew that the giant Pacific octopus is the largest kind of octopus in the world, but I didn't know a lot about octopuses, and the experience inspired me to read a book about them. The book I found was written by two scientists who have been studying octopuses for many years, and I learned a lot of surprising and cool things. For instance, octopuses can **camouflage** themselves better than any other animal because they not only change their colour to match their surroundings, they also change their texture! I also learned that even though octopuses are related to clams, mussels and oysters, they are, in fact, *very* smart. Some collect seashells or coconut shells and then use them

as a kind of suit of armour when they feel threatened. They are also amazing escape artists. An octopus named Inky, who was kept in an aquarium in New Zealand, escaped from his tank, crawled across the floor and then squished himself into a drainpipe, which led him to freedom back in the ocean! Octopuses can fit into *very* small places because they don't have bones. Imagine the small spaces *you* could fit into if you didn't have bones.

Octopuses have three hearts and blue blood, and each of their eight arms has a cluster of nerve cells that is kind of like a brain. This means that their arms can be doing completely different things at the same time, without any input from the main brain in their head. Wow!

Living in Trash

There is so much human garbage in the ocean now that many different kinds of octopuses have been seen using items such as glass and plastic bottles, tin cans and other human-made debris as places to lay their eggs, to protect themselves from predators and to camouflage their dens. Scientists from Brazil and Italy did a study on the ways in which octopuses use human garbage and how common it is. They found that sometimes octopuses are harmed by using dangerous garbage such as sharp glass, which can cut them, and car batteries, which can leak poisonous chemicals. Studies such as this illustrate how important it is to keep our trash out of the ocean. Always make sure you recycle, put your garbage in a garbage can, and produce less garbage by using reusable water bottles, straws, cutlery and shopping bags.

Whitcomberd

What Is Seaweed?   **17**

Seaweed for the Health of Our Earth!

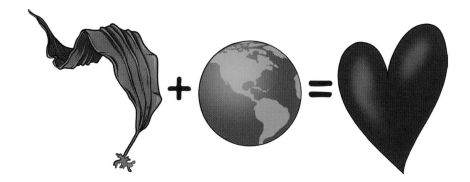

Did you know that seaweeds help keep our Earth healthy? Here are some of the ways seaweed is an Earth helper:

Seaweed produces *lots* of oxygen

As you now know, seaweeds are algae, and some algae are very tiny and can only be seen using a microscope. Well, if you take all the algae in the world, from the tiny microalgae to the largest kelp, they produce a *lot* of oxygen. Scientists estimate that between 50 to 80 percent of all the oxygen on our planet is produced by algae! That means that at least every second breath you take was made by algae! Every animal on Earth needs oxygen to breathe.

Seaweed helps protect the Earth from climate change

Seaweeds absorb a gas called carbon dioxide because they use it when they photosynthesize. If there is too much carbon dioxide in the air, it can make the Earth too hot. Scientists estimate that algae (remember, this includes all seaweeds) absorb one-third of all the carbon dioxide in our atmosphere. That is a lot of carbon dioxide!

Seaweed cleans the water

Seaweeds make the water cleaner in areas where they grow. Seaweeds are like environmental superheroes!

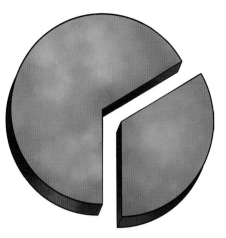

Amount of carbon dioxide that algae absorb, which removes it from the atmosphere.

Seaweed for the Health of Our Bodies!

Seaweed is one of the healthiest foods you can eat! Seaweeds are similar to vegetables in many ways, but instead of growing on land, they grow in the sea. Some people even call seaweed "sea vegetables." Like vegetables, seaweeds are very healthy and are full of vitamins and minerals.

Seaweed is very healthy because it:

- is high in vitamins, including vitamins A, B, C, D, E and K. That's a *lot* of vitamins! What are vitamins good for? Among other things, they keep our blood, bones and muscles healthy and help us to heal wounds and get better quickly after being sick.
- has a higher concentration of minerals than any other food on Earth! Up to 39 percent of the weight of dried

Phyco-fact

Remember all those vitamins and minerals that are in seaweed? Well, fruits and vegetables also need those to grow. Adding seaweed to your compost and garden soil can help you grow beautiful and nutritious fruits and veggies!

Seaweeds are nature's superstars!

Nicole Yamamoto

seaweed is minerals. They even contain very rare minerals that are not found in fruits and vegetables. We need minerals to keep our brains, bones, skin, hair, eyes and heart healthy. We also need minerals to be able to think, digest our food, move our bodies and so much more.

- is a great source of protein, which we need to grow and to repair muscles and bones.
- contains substances called essential fatty acids, which help keep our brain, heart and blood vessels healthy.

Seaweed is a salty, delicious and healthy snack. *Harbour Publishing*

- helps make our skin healthy.
- contains something called **sodium alginate**, which helps our body get rid of toxins. Toxins are poisonous substances that our bodies absorb in small amounts in our daily life.
- contains some very healthy substances that are not found in any other food. Scientists who study some of these substances, such as **fucoidan**, **fucoxanthin** and phlorotannins, believe they can help protect us from certain kinds of diseases.
- has been used as a medicine to treat many different types of illnesses in places around the world. In some places, including Egypt, seaweeds have been used as medicine for more than a thousand years!

We can drink it! Christina Symons

We can heal our bodies with it!

We can make music with it!

We can use it to feel relaxed and to make our skin soft!

We can admire its beauty.

We can use it in our gardens to make healthy soil for plants.

We can eat it!

We can even make glasses with it!

We can make baskets with it! This kelp basket was made by artist Patty Dowler.

Harvesting Seaweed

Harvesting Seaweed Safely

If you are going to harvest your own seaweed, here are some ways to help ensure that you harvest it safely.

- *Know what the tide is doing before you go.* It is very important to know if the tide is coming in (this is called a **flooding tide**) or going out (this is called an **ebbing tide**). On some beaches, when the tide is very high, the path you took onto the beach could be underwater when you want to leave! The safest time to harvest is *before* the low tide.

- *Seaweed is slippery!* Be very careful walking over seaweed as it is *very* slippery. Wear boots or shoes with good treads. Remember to walk around the seaweed, not on it, whenever possible.

- *Don't harvest from areas that are polluted.* Only harvest seaweed from a clean area. Ask an adult if a particular beach is a safe area to harvest. It should be far from sewage outfalls, shipyards and other industrial areas.

- *Don't eat any seaweeds you do not recognize.* Never eat any seaweed unless you are sure it is a kind that is safe to eat.

Opposite: A seaweed called Turkish towel in wonderful condition, found washed up on the beach.

Tide Websites

The Canadian government's website shows the time of the high and low tides for many coastal areas of Canada: tides.gc.ca. In the United States, go to: tidesandcurrents.noaa.gov.

Harvesting Respectfully

If you live in the traditional territory of a First Nation, be sure to respect any harvesting regulations they have in your area.

This beach has lots of a brown seaweed called winged kelp, so it would be okay to harvest some pieces from here.

Get Ready to Harvest

Before you harvest seaweed, you need to know where to find the seaweed you are looking for. Once you have found a beach where lots of the seaweed you want to harvest is growing, find out the time that the tide will be low on the day you would like to harvest. It is also good to know how the seaweed you want to harvest reproduces. Some seaweeds, like winged kelp, have separate reproductive structures that should be left alone so that the seaweed can reproduce. *Remember not to harvest in national or state / provincial parks.*

- Folding knife or scissors
- Bucket or plastic bag (large resealable plastic bags work well)
- Boots or shoes with good treads that you don't mind getting wet, or wetsuit booties

Sometimes you need a wetsuit to keep you warm if you are harvesting seaweeds that grow in deeper water, but please do not go into deep water unless you are with an adult.

A baby bull kelp.

How to Be a Sustainable Seaweed Harvester

There are some very important things to know before you harvest seaweed, in order to harvest **sustainably**. Doing something sustainably means doing it in a mindful way that ensures the balance of the ecosystem will be preserved. When we harvest seaweed sustainably, the seaweed can keep growing, much like grass keeps growing after it has been cut. The most important thing to remember is to leave seaweed attached to the rock it is growing on and only cut some of it. Just like your hair after a haircut, the seaweed will grow back. If you rip seaweed from the rock it is attached to, it will not grow back and will die.

Bleach weed, *Prionitis* spp.

- *Never take more seaweed than you need.* It is very important to only take the amount of seaweed you can use, so you don't waste any.
- *If you only see a little bit of one kind of seaweed, let it grow.* If there is only a little bit of a particular kind of seaweed growing in the area you are exploring, don't harvest any of that kind of seaweed. Make sure when you harvest that there is lots of the kind you are harvesting on the beach.
- *Be gentle in the intertidal zone.* Walk gently and carefully in the intertidal zone, and try not to walk on top of seaweed that is attached to rocks on the beach at low tide. Remember: there are creatures such as crabs, sea stars and anemones hiding in the seaweed!

Are Any Seaweeds Poisonous?

While there are no seaweeds that are poisonous, there *are* seaweeds that you should not eat. Some seaweeds you should *not eat* are:

Acid Kelp

Acid kelp belongs to the brown seaweed group, but it isn't actually a kelp. This seaweed contains something called **sulphuric acid**, which can upset your stomach and burn or sting your mouth the same way eating something with too much vinegar can. Another important thing to know about acid kelp: if you put it in the same bucket as your other seaweeds, it will cause them to turn slimy.

Stringy Acid Weed

Stringy acid weed belongs to the same **genus** as acid kelp, *Desmarestia*, and like acid kelp it contains sulphuric acid and should not be eaten.

Bleach Weed

Bleach weed contains high amounts of something called **chlorine**. Chlorine is used in household cleaners, and even in swimming pools, to kill germs. While small amounts of chlorine are not harmful, too much is poisonous. While

Flattened acid kelp, *Desmarestia* spp. (flattened form)

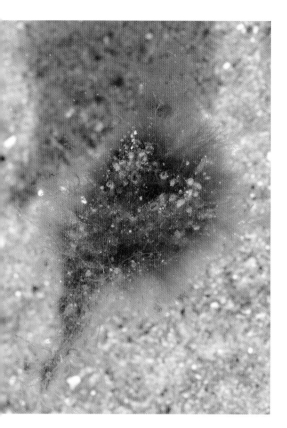

Stringy acid weed, *Desmarestia* spp.
(cylindrical form) *Christine Young*

bleach weed doesn't contain enough chlorine to be poisonous, it is still not good to eat.

Salvaging Seaweed

Sometimes very fresh pieces of seaweed wash up on the beach, and you can just gather them. Harvesting seaweed this way is called **salvaging**, and it is a very sustainable way to harvest seaweed. To determine if the seaweed is still fresh enough to keep, you need to *look* at it, *smell* it and *touch* it.

- *Look at the seaweed:* The colour of the seaweed should be the same throughout the whole piece of seaweed, without any white or clear patches. If parts of it are white or clear, it is not fresh anymore.
- *Smell the seaweed:* When you smell it, it should smell briny, like the salty smell of the beach at low tide. If it smells bad, it is not fresh anymore and you shouldn't

Harvesting dulse. Notice that lots of the seaweed is still attached to the rock.

Cut Your Seaweed Safely

When you use a knife to cut seaweed, make sure an adult is with you, and be safe: always cut away from your body and hands, and never walk or run with an open knife.

Phyco-fact

Seaweeds are among the fastest-growing living things on the planet!

use it, except to put on your garden or in your compost. Have you ever smelled rotten seaweed? Peeeeeeyew!!!

- *Touch the seaweed:* When you touch it, the seaweed should feel smooth and jelly-like, similar to the liquid inside an aloe vera plant. It should not feel slimy and definitely should not leave a brown colour on your skin. If it does, it is not good to eat.

Rinsing Your Seaweed

If you are harvesting your own seaweed for food, it is very important to carefully rinse it. Eating seaweed full of sand is not very enjoyable and can even hurt your teeth. If you don't rinse your seaweed, you may end up eating creatures such as tiny shellfish or isopods without even knowing it! The best way to clean your seaweed is to carefully rinse each piece, one at a time, in clean seawater before you leave the beach. You can also rinse your seaweed at home by filling up a large pot with tap water and adding a teaspoon of sea salt. Next, take a piece of seaweed in both hands and submerge it three or four times, then hang it to dry and move on to the next piece until all of your seaweed has been well rinsed. If your water becomes too sandy, empty the pot and refill.

Drying Seaweed

Drying seaweed is a great way to preserve it. When we preserve food, we prepare the food so that it stays good for a long time. Some ways to preserve food include canning it in jars, salting it, freezing it and drying it. Drying seaweed is the best way to preserve it, and people have been drying seaweed for thousands of years!

When I harvest seaweeds that are covered by water, like winged kelp, I can just give them a little scrub as I go. Seaweeds that grow on the shore and are exposed at low tide, such as sea lettuce and black nori, require much more careful rinsing.

How to Dry Seaweed:

- You can hang larger seaweeds such as kelp on a clothesline outside, or even on tree branches. Once they are dry enough that they have stopped dripping, you can move them inside and hang them from a wooden clothes-drying rack or plastic hangers. They usually take two to three days to dry. Do not hang your seaweed on anything metal because the metal will rust and get onto the seaweed, making it unsafe to eat.
- For smaller seaweeds like nori, dulse and sea lettuce, you can spread them on racks inside your house to dry. Once they feel dry on top, flip them over. They usually take one to two days to dry.

Bull kelp hanging to dry in my special seaweed-drying shop. In the photo on the left, the bull kelp is still very wet. In the photo on the right, it is almost dry. Notice how the seaweed's colour changes and becomes darker when it is dry.

Bull kelp blades hanging to dry in pine tree branches.

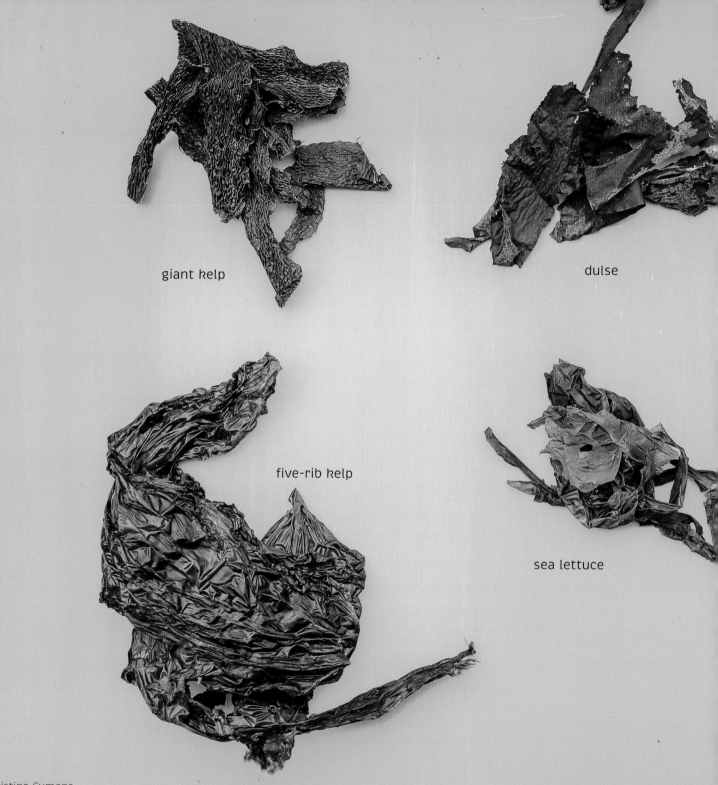

giant kelp

dulse

five-rib kelp

sea lettuce

Christina Symons

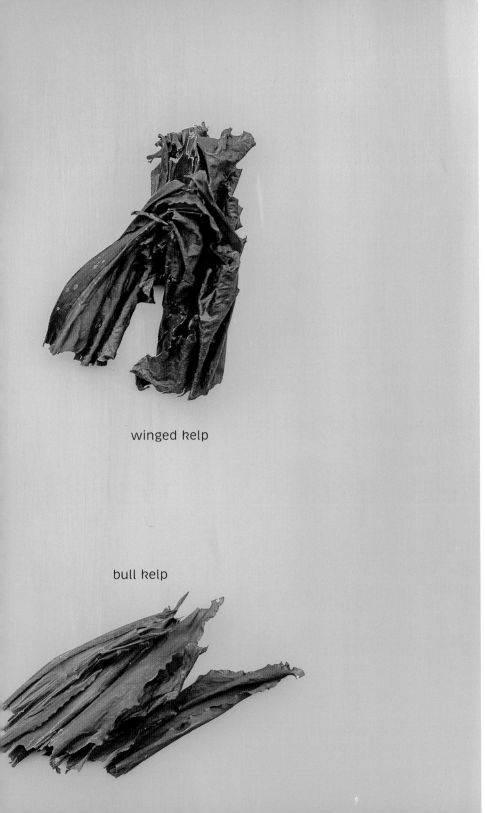

winged kelp

bull kelp

How to Store Seaweed

Once your seaweed is dry, you can store it in glass jars with lids or resealable plastic bags. Your seaweed will stay good like this for at least one year.

Christina Symons

Giving Back to the Ocean

When you take seaweed, think about how you can give something back. That way, it is kind of like an exchange or a trade, and it is good for both you *and* the seaweed. Here are some ways you can help keep seaweeds—and our ocean—healthy.

- Talk to your family and friends about how awesome and amazing seaweed is.
- Pick up garbage on the beach.
- Join a group that helps protect the ocean, or form your own.
- Make sure any soap and cleaning products you use in your home are safe for the ocean.
- Try to use less plastic, especially plastic that you only use once and then throw away, like plastic water bottles or other drink containers.
- Participate in a community beach clean-up or organize your own.

Do you have any other ideas of ways you can give back to the ocean?

Organize Your Own Beach Clean-Up!

Plastic pollution in the ocean can be harmful to many sea creatures. Picking up plastic garbage and other debris such as Styrofoam on the beach is one way to help protect the ocean and the creatures who live in it. Many communities have beach clean-ups, or you can organize your own. Ask your friends if they want to help you get things rolling.

For your beach clean-up you will need:

- A pair of work gloves
- A package of large black garbage bags
- A package of large clear garbage bags
- Paper and markers

Steps for organizing a beach clean-up:

1. Pick a date and a time for your beach clean-up. A time when the tide is low works best, because that's when more of the beach is exposed, and when floating garbage is left on the beach. When the tide comes back in, debris on the beach that floats will be taken back out to sea with the tide. To find out when the tide will be low, visit a website that tells you the times of the high and low tides for your area.

2. Make a poster. Be sure to include the date, time and location of your beach clean-up. It is also good to include a reminder that people should bring their own work gloves. You can draw your favourite ocean creature or seaweed on the poster as well! Once you are done, make several copies of your poster and put them up at places like your school, the grocery store or a café. Some neighbourhoods have a bulletin board near community mailboxes, which is also a good place to put up your poster. You can also take a photo of your poster and ask an adult to share it on social media.

3. Bring one package of black garbage bags and one package of clear garbage bags to your beach clean-up. Give one clear bag and one black bag to every group who comes to your beach clean-up. The clear bag is for recyclables, such as plastic water

bottles, drink containers, glass bottles and cans. The black bag is for garbage that can't be recycled, such as Styrofoam, candy wrappers, toothbrushes and small bits of plastic. After the beach clean-up is finished, you can take the recyclables to a recycling depot, or add them to your family's recycling.

4. Make sure to put your work gloves on before you start picking up debris from the beach.

5. Document your beach clean-up. You can document the clean-up by taking photos of the beach before the clean-up and after, and photos of all the garbage that was collected. This may inspire others to do a clean-up at another beach.

6. *If there is anything on the beach that is unsafe, such as sharp glass, needles or aerosol cans, DO NOT pick these items up. Instead, if there is an adult at your beach clean-up, let them know where the unsafe item is. If no adult is with you, leave the items where they are and tell an adult later.*

SolStock

Otter Rock

Years ago, when my daughters were still too young to attend school and would come with me to the beach for the *Alaria* harvest, I named a particular rock Otter Rock. On all but the lowest tides of the year, Otter Rock is like a little island, with different amounts of it sticking out of the water depending on the height of the tide. More often than not, my daughters and I would see otters hauling themselves up on this rock, much like seals or sea lions do. Oftentimes it wasn't just one, but a family of otters. One time we counted seven otters, all lumped together on that one not-too-big rock!

The type of otters we would see are called river otters. They are related to sea otters, the very cute, furry otters who spend almost their entire life at sea, but they are not as fluffy. They frequently run along the shore by the water's edge and can travel quite far on land.

One sunny day in April, I was out in my seaweed garden harvesting *Alaria* and my nephew, Grayson, was on the beach with my dog, Jazz. I heard him call me from the beach: "Aunt Mandy, what's that?" I turned my gaze to where he was pointing, out into the water. I saw the quick surface and dive of the sleek and almost snake-like movements of an otter.

"It's an otter," I yelled back across the water. "It's probably heading to that rock." I pointed to Otter Rock. Sure enough, a few seconds later the otter pulled itself up onto the rock.

"Oh yeah!" my nephew replied excitedly. He sat on a large boulder by the water's edge watching the otter.

I got back to my harvesting, finding a long, beautiful blade of *Alaria*, pulling it up gently from underneath the clear water and cutting it carefully to ensure a good portion of it stayed anchored to the rock its holdfast was gripped onto. A few minutes later, the otter dove back into the water and swam to the beach. Grayson gave me the play-by-play of the otter's whereabouts.

"He's on the beach now!" "He's back in the water!" "There's two of them!"

I was about halfway between the beach and Otter Rock, in about waist-deep water, when the otter climbed back up onto Otter Rock. This time it had a big flatfish in its mouth, which it laid onto the rock. Holding it in place with a paw, the otter began eating the fish, and I could hear it tearing off pieces with its teeth and then chewing it up with gusto.

I momentarily forgot about the piece of *Alaria* in my hand, mesmerized by the scene in front of me. I turned to look back toward the beach to see if Grayson was seeing this. He had lost interest in keeping up with the otter's movements and was looking for crabs underneath rocks. "Look!" I said enthusiastically, trying to be loud enough for him to hear me but quiet enough to not scare away the otter. "It's eating a flatfish." Grayson forgot about the crabs and immediately trained his eyes on the fish-eating otter. After another minute or two, I finally pried my eyes away from the otter, still devouring the fish, and returned to harvesting *Alaria*.

Not a minute later, I saw a huge dark shape appear above me in my peripheral vision. I quickly snapped my head up in time to see a bald eagle just a stone's throw above my head. Its wingspan was as wide as a tall man as it swooshed past me toward Otter Rock. Panic gripped me for a second as I imagined the eagle grabbing the fish-eating otter in its large talons. Twice I have seen a bald eagle swoop quickly down and clutch an unsuspecting floating seagull from the water. Once, on the trail to my *Alaria* garden, I saw one grab a rabbit and fly high into the sky with the rabbit in its talons.

Kate Woods

Even though an otter is larger than a seagull or a rabbit, and much heavier, it still seemed like a possibility.

The eagle did indeed land on Otter Rock, its outstretched legs lined with black feathers that made it look like it was wearing leg warmers, and slowly tucked its massive wings against its body. I breathed a sigh of relief when I saw that the otter was no longer there. It must have seen the eagle coming, like I did, and decided to slink back into the sea. The fish, however, was still there, and the eagle dug into its stolen meal.

A few seconds before, I had been captivated by the sight of an otter eating a flatfish. Now, still standing in waist-deep water with my bag of *Alaria*, I watched a bald eagle from just a short distance away holding the fish in place on the rock with its large talon and ripping off pieces with its sharp beak. Nature was putting on an awesome display today!

I turned back around toward the beach to ensure that Grayson was seeing this spectacular show of nature. His eyes were glued on Otter Rock as he shouted at me and pointed: "A bald eagle!"

Over the twenty years I have been a seaweed harvester, I have had many special experiences with the animals who live in the ocean and the intertidal zone. These experiences are gifts from the Earth for which I am deeply grateful. I like to think that if you listen carefully to your heart and do what you love, not only will the world appreciate what you give to it, but it will give something back to you, often when you least expect it.

The common name for *Alaria* is winged kelp, but I like to call it by its genus name, *Alaria*, because I think it is such a beautiful name. It comes from the Greek word for "winged."

Brown Seaweeds

The brown seaweed group includes seaweeds such as giant kelp, bull kelp, winged kelp, oarweed, Atlantic kombu and rockweed. Seaweeds in the brown group can be dark brown, light brown, greenish brown or yellowish brown. Every kind of kelp belongs to the brown seaweed group.

Opposite, top left to bottom right: bull kelp, *Nereocystis luetkeana*; winged kelp with sunflower star, *Alaria marginata*; rockweed, *Fucus distichus (Emma Geiger)*; oarweed, *Laminaria digitata*; giant kelp, *Macrocystis pyrifera*.

Feather boa, *Egregia menziesii*

Scientific Names

All seaweeds have a **scientific name**. This name consists of two words. The first word is the name of the **genus** the seaweed belongs to. Seaweeds that belong to the same genus are very closely related. The second word is the name of the **species**. There can be more than one seaweed in the same genus, but every seaweed has its own unique species name. It is not only seaweeds that have scientific names. Scientists try to name every living thing on Earth this way. Why do they do this? Because the scientific name shows how living things are related to each other. For example, two seaweeds that are in the same genus are more closely related than seaweeds that are not in the same genus. Another reason scientific names are important is that while there can be several common names for a species, in several different languages, there is only one scientific name. For example, the brown seaweed *Alaria marginata* has all of these common names: winged kelp, wild wakame, ribbon kelp, angel wing kelp and broad-winged kelp. And those are only the English common names. It has more common names in other languages, such as languages of the Coast Salish peoples. Additionally, two or more types of seaweed may both have the same common name. By using scientific names, phycologists (scientists who study seaweeds) from around the world, who speak many different languages, can indicate to one another the specific seaweed they are studying.

Phyco-fact

There are about two thousand species of brown algae, also called **phaeophytes**, in the world.

Bull Kelp

Nereocystis luetkeana

Bull kelp is in the brown seaweed group. It is one of my very favourite seaweeds. It looks like a mermaid if you see it under-water. Its stipe is a long, hollow tube that looks like the body and ends in a big, round bulb that looks like the head. The blades flow behind it in the current, like long, beautiful hair.

Here are some of my favourite facts about bull kelp:

A young bull kelp.

- Bull kelp is the second-largest seaweed in the whole world and can grow to be forty metres long. That is the length of six orcas swimming in a row!
- Bull kelp is one of the fastest-growing things on Earth and can grow longer than your foot in just one day!
- Bull kelp can stretch by almost half of its length when being pulled by strong ocean swells and currents.
- Kelp crabs are a kind of crab that has evolved to live on bull kelp. I see kelp crabs almost every time I harvest bull kelp.
- The stipe of bull kelp makes a great musical instrument! If you blow into the wide end of the stipe, it makes a sound like a didgeridoo.
- Bull kelp is one of the healthiest foods you can eat. It's salty and delicious!

Bull kelp reproduces by releasing large rectangular patches, called **spore patches**, from some of its blades. After these

The spore patch has already dropped out of the blade here.

This spore patch will be the next one to drop from the blade.

Spore patch on a blade of bull kelp.

spore patches are released, you can see large, rectangular holes in the blades of the bull kelp where they used to be. The spore patches are filled with **spores**, which are cells that can grow into a brand-new bull kelp.

Eating Bull Kelp

Bull kelp tastes like the ocean: salty and tingly. I love to use it as a seasoning by grinding it up into flakes and sprinkling it on top of pasta, eggs, chili, soup, salad and especially popcorn. It also contains tons of nutrients, which your body needs to be healthy. Bull kelp has vitamins A, B, C, D, E and K. That is more kinds of vitamins than fruits and vegetables have! It is also full of minerals such as calcium and iron, which you need for strong bones and healthy blood. Bull kelp is both delicious *and* healthy.

blades

stipe

Bull kelp blades and stipe.

Bull Kelp Sea-soning

Ingredients

Bull kelp, dried

Directions

Grind bull kelp in a blender until it is in small flakes, about
15 or 20 seconds. I put my Bull Kelp Sea-soning into a pretty
shell. I sometimes collect shells at the beach, wash them
and then use them as little bowls. You can put your dish
of Sea-soning on your table for mealtimes
and sprinkle it on top of food for
a delicious, salty taste that is
full of healthy vitamins and
minerals.

Bull Kelp Sea-soning is
salty and delicious on
popcorn! *Christina Symons*

Cold and Flu Fighter!

Seaweed has lots of vitamin C. This vitamin helps our bodies fight off colds and flus and helps us get better after we have been sick.

Palm Trees in the Sea

This seaweed, which is in the brown seaweed group, is called sea palm (*Postelsia palmaeformis*) and looks like a small palm tree. It grows in the Pacific Northwest and can withstand the force of large, powerful waves crashing onto it.

Alaria marginata

Winged kelp is another seaweed in the brown seaweed group. Winged kelp grows in the low intertidal zone and the subtidal zone. The scientific name for winged kelp that grows in the North Pacific Ocean is *Alaria marginata*. The scientific name for winged kelp that grows in the North Atlantic Ocean is *Alaria esculenta*. Winged kelp has a thick line running down the middle of it called a midrib, which can appear almost golden when you see it underwater. Near the holdfast, the part of the seaweed that is anchored to a rock, are small, leaf-shaped parts called sporophylls. Sporophylls are the reproductive parts of winged kelp and contain spores that will grow into new winged kelps. When harvesting winged kelp, it is very important to leave the sporophylls attached

Seaweed for Healthy Bones

Calcium is an important mineral for healthy bones. Winged kelp is one of the highest sources of calcium in the world!

Harvesting winged kelp. *Mahina Burley*

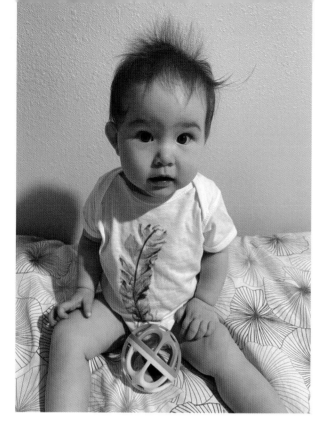

Above: Winged kelp is such a beautiful seaweed it has even made its way into the fashion industry! *Tien Bui*

Right top: Winged kelp hanging to dry in my seaweed shop.

Right bottom: A blood star with winged kelp.

Parts of winged kelp. *Emma Geiger*

This is me holding a large winged kelp that is anchored to a rock. In my left hand I am holding the blade and in my right hand I am holding a sporophyll, which is the reproductive part of this seaweed. *Emma Geiger*

so that new seaweeds can grow. The part of the seaweed that has the midrib, which is called the blade, can be cut and eaten.

Like bull kelp, winged kelp is one of the healthiest foods in the world. It is loaded with minerals and vitamins and, like other brown seaweeds, contains some special substances that are not found in any other foods. Two of these substances are called fucoidan and fucoxanthin, and scientists that have studied them think they can help protect us from certain diseases such as cancer, diabetes and heart disease. In laboratory conditions, these substances have shown activity associated with the prevention of these diseases.

Here is the recipe for one of my favourite soups, which I make with winged kelp. It can also be made with a seaweed called wakame.

Mermaid's Miso Soup

Ingredients

- About 10 grams (1 big piece) winged kelp or wakame, fresh or dried
- 4 cups (950 mL) water
- 2 Tbsp (30 mL) miso paste
- ½ package (about 125 grams) silken tofu, cut into small cubes
- 2 scallions, chopped small

Directions

1. Use clean scissors to cut winged kelp into small pieces.
2. Pour water into a pot and bring to a boil on the stove (make sure an adult helps you with the stove).
3. Turn heat down to medium-low, add kelp, then simmer for 10 minutes. Remove pot from heat and turn off stove.
4. Add miso and stir until well mixed.
5. Divide cubes of tofu between small soup bowls and pour soup into bowls then garnish with scallions.

Serves 4

Sea cauliflower (*Leathesia marina*) is a
small brown seaweed that grows in the
Pacific Ocean along the west coast of
North America. It has a very odd shape
and looks like a human brain!

Bear Beach

One of the most exciting parts of being a seaweed harvester on Vancouver Island is that I not only get to see amazing sea creatures, but I also get to spend time with some awesome land animals. One day, while I was harvesting winged kelp, a bear arrived at the beach and decided to stay! You need to be *very* respectful and careful of bears, of course, because they can be dangerous. This bear was quite a long way down the beach from me and not between me and the trail to my car. The bear was medium-sized, had long legs and was a little skinnier than other bears I had seen. I kept a close eye on him as I harvested seaweed. The whole time I harvested, the bear was fully immersed in pawing and nosing through piles of rotting seaweed that had washed up on the beach, apparently searching meticulously for something. I wondered what he was looking for. Little crabs? Sand fleas? His favourite kind of seaweed?

Whenever I see a bear I feel a mix of excitement, nervousness and wonderment. Bears are grand and powerful creatures, and I always feel like I am receiving a special gift—when I get to see one—from a safe distance, of course.

The next morning, I headed back to the beach to harvest winged kelp again and guess who I saw? *The same bear.* "Wow," I thought. "I go to work with a bear!" I laughed to myself as I imagined a bear sitting at a desk in an office

This is the bear that stayed for three days at the beach where I harvest seaweed!

Brown Seaweeds **59**

building. Just like the day before, the bear was very busy pawing and nosing through piles of seaweed.

The same bear was at the beach again the following day, the *third day* in a row I had seen him. As I dipped my hand into the ocean, pulling up a long, beautiful blade of winged kelp, I thought about how fortunate I was to have a job where I get to see such incredible animals.

I didn't see the bear again after the third day, but I often found myself thinking about him while I harvested seaweed on that beach—*the bear's beach*. I hoped that wherever he was, he was getting enough to eat and was having the best life that a bear can have.

Feather Boa

Egregia menziesii

This is feather boa. Not the kind you wear to a party, though. This feather boa belongs to the brown seaweed group and is also a kelp. It looks like a seaweed version of a feather boa, which is how it got its name. When I see it at the beach, I imagine mermaids wearing it around their necks when attending an underwater party. Feather boa can grow up to fifteen metres (almost fifty feet) long. That is as long as a whale shark, the largest fish in the sea! Feather boa only grows in the North Pacific Ocean.

Fresh Feather Boa Fronds

Take a pair of scissors and trim off some of the small fronds that grow from the midrib of a feather boa. Make sure to leave the seaweed attached, so that it will continue to grow. Rinse the fronds that you cut, and then you can eat them plain or add them to soup or a salad for a taste of the ocean.

Feather boa, *Egregia menziesii*.

Emma Geiger

A long piece of feather boa!

Left: Regular feather boa.

Right: Mermaid-style feather boa.

Artur Jany

Parts of a feather boa.

These air-filled sacs are called **floats** or **pneumatocysts**, and they make the feather boa float at the surface of the water. This helps the seaweed capture more sunlight for photosynthesis, which makes it grow.

Ecosystem Superstars

Seaweeds are called **primary producers**. What does it mean if something is a primary producer? It means that it can photosynthesize: it can use energy from sunlight to make nutrients from carbon dioxide and water in order to grow. Imagine if instead of eating your regular lunch, you could use sunlight to make your lunch instead! Well, seaweeds (and plants as well) can do that. Because they can do that, they are the primary, or original, source of energy, or food, in their ecosystem. Everything in an ecosystem depends on primary producers. I will show you what I mean in the following illustration of a **food chain**. A food chain shows the order in which organisms depend on one another for food, starting with a primary producer. In this food chain, bull kelp is the primary producer and therefore is at the *bottom* of the food chain. Everything in this food chain depends on the bull kelp.

Do you see how all the animals in the food chain need the bull kelp? For example, even though the Dungeness crab doesn't eat bull kelp, it still depends on the bull kelp because the food it does eat—limpets—eats bull kelp.

A bull kelp uses energy from the sun to make it grow into a large seaweed. A limpet eats the kelp. A Dungeness crab eats the limpet. A sunflower star eats the Dungeness crab. A sea otter eats the sunflower star. An orca eats the sea otter.

Known as "soda straws" on the Pacific coast and "sausage seaweed" on the Atlantic coast, this cylindrical brown seaweed consists of hollow tubes that narrow between sections, much like a string of sausages. Its scientific name is *Scytosiphon* sp.

Giant Kelp

Macrocystis pyrifera

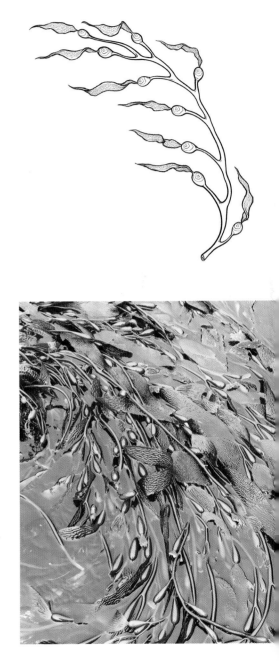

Giant kelp (*Macrocystis pyrifera*) belongs to the brown seaweed group and is the largest seaweed in the world! It can grow to fifty-three metres (174 feet) tall, which is taller than Niagara Falls and almost as tall as the tallest red cedar tree! It is a **perennial** seaweed, which means that it doesn't die in the winter like many other seaweeds and plants. Instead, it can live for several years. Giant kelp forms large underwater kelp forests that provide a **habitat**, or home, for many kinds of fish, jellyfish, shellfish, crabs and **marine mammals** such as seals and sea lions. Giant kelp grows in the Pacific Ocean from Alaska to Baja California and in the Southern Ocean off the coast of South America and Australia.

Giant kelp is also delicious to eat! Because it grows deep in the ocean, it is usually harvested by boat. If you live near the ocean in places where giant kelp grows, you can also harvest it by salvaging. When you salvage seaweed, you can collect kinds that grow in very deep water without even getting your feet wet! If you go to the beach on a day when there are very large waves, or after it has been very windy, you will often find giant kelp that is still very fresh washed right up on the beach! Do you remember how to check if seaweed that has been washed up on the beach is still fresh enough to use? If you forget, have a look at the section "Salvaging Seaweed" on page 30.

Giant kelp looks like towering underwater trees. *Maxwel Hohn*

Phyco-fact

Small fish called herring often lay their eggs on giant kelp. When the giant kelp is dried, the herring eggs remain stuck to it. In some cultures, this is considered a gourmet snack! It is called *roe-on-kelp* in English and *komochi kombu* in Japanese. In Xaat Kíl, the ancestral language of the Haida people, it is called K'aaw.

Roe-on-kelp. *Tien Bui*

Eating Giant Kelp

I love to eat giant kelp with fish such as halibut or lingcod. I just put a big piece of seaweed on top of the fish when I cook it. It is tangy and delicious with rice. I also love to make kelp chips. They are salty and satisfying after a long day of harvesting seaweed in the frigid waters of the Pacific Northwest.

Kelp Chips

Be sure to have an adult help you with frying!

Ingredients

- About 30 grams dry giant kelp
  (you can also use winged kelp)
- 1 tsp (5 mL) garlic powder
- 1 tsp (5 mL) fresh ground pepper
- 1 Tbsp (15 mL) coconut oil

Directions

1. Using clean scissors, cut giant kelp into 4 cm by 4 cm squares.
2. Put squares into a bowl and toss with garlic powder and pepper.
3. Heat coconut oil in a skillet on medium heat.
4. Once the oil is hot, carefully spread kelp squares in a single layer in the pan. (It is best to let an adult do this part as the oil can splash from the skillet and burn you.)
5. Fry kelp for 1 minute on each side.
6. Remove from skillet with tongs onto a baking sheet lined with absorbent paper towel. Use another paper towel on top of the giant kelp to dab excess oil.
7. Transfer to a bowl and enjoy!

Christina Symons

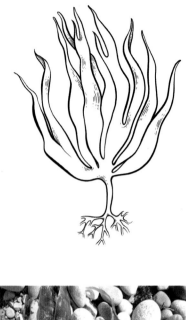

Oarweed

Laminaria digitata

Just as bull kelp and giant kelp form large underwater kelp forests in the North Pacific, oarweed forms kelp forests in the North Atlantic. A big difference, though, is that oarweed is much smaller than bull kelp and giant kelp, so Atlantic kelp forests look more like kelp bushes. Oarweed is a type of kombu and can be used to make flavourful soup stocks. Kombu includes a number of different seaweeds that are related to each other, and that belong to either the *Saccharina* or *Laminaria* genus. In Japan, kombu is used to make dashi, a broth that is used in many different Japanese dishes. If you are cooking beans, you can add a piece of oarweed to your pot to make the beans less likely to cause flatulence. Flatulence is a fancy way of saying "passing gas." On the Atlantic coast, you may sometimes see oarweed sold under the name Atlantic kombu.

Tea of Land and Sea

In the spring I gather spruce tips, which have a wonderful, lemony taste, and then combine them with mint from my garden and winged kelp to make a vitamin- and mineral-rich, immune-enhancing tea. You can try my recipe or create your very own Tea of Land and Sea by combining seaweed and edible herbs and flowers. Always check with an adult before gathering wild plants to make sure they are safe.

Ingredients and Materials

- A small handful of fresh or dried seaweed such as sea lettuce, winged kelp, wakame, feather boa, oarweed or Atlantic kombu, cut into small pieces. If you are using dried seaweed, you don't need as much.
- A small handful of fresh or dried edible herbs and flowers like mint, rosemary, spruce tips, rose petals, calendula, nasturtiums and/or fireweed blossoms. If you are using dried herbs, you don't need as much.
- A teapot
- Boiling water
- A strainer

Christina Symons

Directions

Place your ingredients in a teapot and, with an adult's help, fill with boiling water. Allow to steep for 5 minutes. Strain into cups and enjoy! You can play around with your recipe until you find one that is tasty. It may also change with the seasons, and which seaweeds and herbs are available in your area.

Phyco-fact

Did you know that some seaweeds can have a different shape depending on where they grow? If this seaweed, called five-rib kelp, grows in an area where it is exposed to big waves, it will grow long and skinny. If it grows in an area that is sheltered from big waves, it will grow short and wide. The ability to grow into a certain shape depending on the environmental conditions is called phenotypic plasticity.

My niece, who is part mermaid like me, holding a piece of oarweed in Nova Scotia.

Oarweed has a stipe that feels like very bendy wood and a blade that can reach a length of two metres, which is divided into long finger-like segments.

An Alligator in the Tub!

Five-rib kelp is a large seaweed in the brown group. I made up another name for this seaweed, "alligator kelp," because when you see it in the water, it looks like the back of an alligator or crocodile. I love to bring a large piece of this seaweed into the bath with me. Not only does it make my skin soft, soothe my muscles and help me relax, it also looks like there is an alligator in the tub!

Five-rib kelp, *Costaria costata*

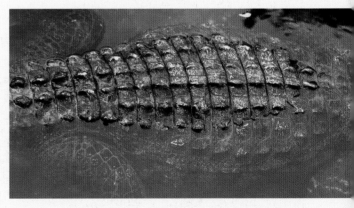

Five-rib kelp reminds me of the back of an alligator or crocodile. *LifeGemz*

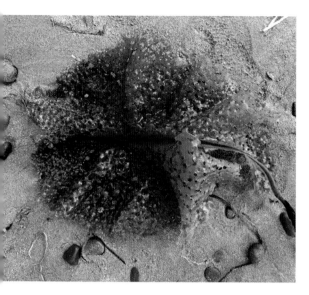

Sieve Kelp

Agarum clathratum

Sieve kelp is a brown seaweed and kelp that grows in the North Atlantic, the North Pacific and the Arctic Ocean. Its blade is covered in little holes. I found this piece in Nova Scotia. Sieve kelp can live to be five or six years old. Sea urchins, who feed on kelp, tend to avoid eating sieve kelp. Scientists think that's because it contains certain chemicals that the urchins don't like.

Sugar Kelp

Saccharina latissima

Sugar kelp grows in both the Atlantic Ocean and the Pacific Ocean and is a popular seaweed to eat. Like its name suggests, it contains natural sugars, which add a subtle sweetness to its salty ocean flavour. Sugar kelp is also cultivated on seaweed farms in the ocean. On the Atlantic coast, sugar kelp is sometimes sold under the names Atlantic kelp and Atlantic kombu. If you want to be sure of what seaweed species you are buying, check for the scientific name.

Atlantic Kombu

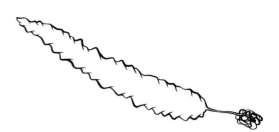

Saccharina longicruris

Atlantic kombu, sometimes called Atlantic kelp, is a brown seaweed and kelp that grows in the North Atlantic Ocean and the Arctic Ocean. It is similar to sugar kelp and is sold as food in the northeastern United States and Atlantic Canada, though it is not as widely available as sugar kelp.

Phyco-fact

In Ireland, people have been bathing with seaweed for centuries, and there are still "seaweed bath houses" in some Irish towns. People bathe in seaweed to soothe sore joints and muscles, improve circulation, induce a feeling of calm and well-being and nourish and soften the skin.

Mermaid Sea Soak

Materials

- About 10 grams dried seaweed (you can use any type of kelp, rainbow seaweed, Turkish towel, Turkish washcloth, Irish moss or rockweed)
- 2 cups (500 mL) Epsom salts
- Glass jar with lid
- 5 drops of your favourite essential oil (my favourites are ylang ylang, grand fir and sandalwood)
- Optional: Scoop-shaped shell such as mussel, clam, oyster or scallop

Directions

1. Cut up dried seaweed into small pieces.
2. Add 2 cups (500 mL) of Epsom salts to glass jar and add in cut up seaweed.
3. Carefully add 5 drops of essential oil.
4. Put lid on jar tightly and shake well.
5. Store near the tub with the lid on.

To Use

While running your bath, add 1 to 2 tablespoons of Mermaid Sea Soak to the water. If you have a pretty shell, use that to scoop it from the jar. Climb into the salty seaweed bath and feel like a mermaid at an underwater spa. Mermaid Sea Soak also makes a lovely gift.

Christina Symons

Christina Symons

Japanese Wire Weed

Sargassum muticum

Japanese wire weed is a seaweed that really loves to travel! Though originally from the waters around the island nation of Japan, this brown seaweed has spread across the globe. Hitching a ride on oyster shells, it can now be found growing in the Atlantic Ocean, the Caribbean Sea, the Mediterranean Sea, the Baltic Sea, and on both sides of the Pacific Ocean. It grows very quickly, and in some areas it will dominate local seaweed species. Japanese wire weed is considered invasive in these areas, because its ability to rapidly spread prevents the local seaweed species from being able to grow. Japanese wire weed is not an edible seaweed.

I found this seaweed, called bladder leaf (*Stephanocystis osmundacea*), in Monterey, California. It has little bladders on its fronds that look like beads. Bladder leaf belongs to the brown seaweed group and grows in the Pacific Ocean from Oregon to Baja California.

Rockweed

There are several species of seaweeds on both the Atlantic and Pacific coasts that are commonly called rockweed. *Fucus distichus* and *Fucus spiralis* grow in both the North Atlantic and the North Pacific, *Ascophyllum nodosum* grows in the North Atlantic and *Fucus vesiculosus* grows in the North Atlantic and the Arctic. *Fucus distichus*, *Fucus spiralis* and *Fucus vesiculosus* are greenish brown and *Ascophyllum nodosum* is a bright yellowish green. All of these species are brown seaweeds known by phycologists as Fucales. Fucales are among the most common, abundant and well-known seaweed species in the Northern Hemisphere.

Rockweed is a very important seaweed in the intertidal ecosystem, particularly on the Atlantic coast, where it is the dominant intertidal species on sheltered or partly sheltered rocky shores. Many creatures find shelter underneath the protective cover of rockweed, and it is a common place for some animals to lay their eggs because it provides shelter from the hot sun and from predators who may want to eat them. There are several companies on the Atlantic coast that harvest large amounts of rockweed, which is then sold as fertilizer, as an additive to feed for cows and sheep and as a nutritional supplement.

Most species of rockweed have bladders that you can pop. In some species, these bladders are the reproductive structures and contain eggs and sperm. In species such as *Fucus distichus*, *Fucus spiralis* and *Fucus vesiculosus*, the

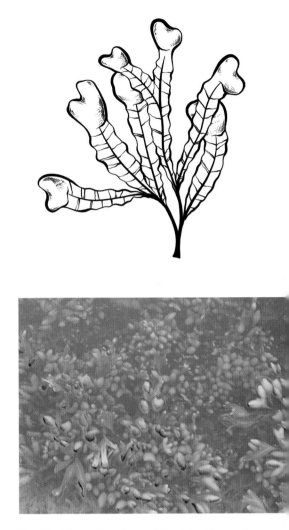

The bladders of rockweed float to the surface in shallow water.

Fucus distichus

Fucus spiralis

bladders are filled with a gelatinous liquid that feels like aloe vera gel. This liquid is a natural sunscreen that protects the seaweed's tiny reproductive cells from being harmed by the sun. You can rub this gel onto your skin to help prevent you from getting a sunburn. If you do get a sunburn or any kind of burn, it can also help to cool and heal your skin.

Common Types of Rockweed

Fucus distichus grows on rocks in the mid-intertidal zone of shores that are sheltered or partly sheltered from open ocean waves.

Fucus spiralis grows in the high intertidal zone of sheltered rocky shores.

On the east coast of Canada and the northeastern coast of the United States, *Ascophyllum nodosum* is a very important species for the health of the intertidal zone. It protects many little sea creatures such as crabs, eels and small fish from being eaten by predators and from drying out in the hot sun.

Fucus vesiculosus is also called bladderwrack, especially in western Europe, where it has been used as a medicine for centuries. A tincture (liquid extract) made from bladderwrack was traditionally used to treat many kinds of illnesses, including viral and bacterial infections, iodine deficiency and stomach maladies. This seaweed is still sold in health-food stores in capsule form.

Ascophyllum nodosum

This species of rockweed, *Ascophyllum nodosum*, covers large swaths of the intertidal zone in Nova Scotia.

Brown Seaweeds **83**

All-Natural Sunscreen

Many seaweeds have been discovered to protect against sun damage. They have developed this ability in order to protect their sensive gametes, the seaweed's reproductive cells. Scientists are starting to test different seaweeds to see what their SPF (sun protection factor) is. One seaweed was found to have an SPF of approximately 22 percent!

1. Carefully cut some rockweed tips, the part of the seaweed you can pop, being careful to leave the rest of the seaweed attached to its rock. Sometimes you can find rockweed that has been washed up on the beach.
2. Break open the tip and rub the gel onto your face and shoulders or other areas you want to protect from getting a sunburn.

You can apply the gel inside rockweed as a natural and coral-safe sunscreen. Unfortunately, most regular sunscreens contain a number of chemicals that are harmful to coral reefs and other marine life.

The tips of rockweed contain a gelatinous substance that is soothing to the skin and helps to prevent sunburn.

Can You Say *Fucus vesiculosus*?!

Scientific names can be hard to remember (and say!), but they are also very useful.

Rockweed is a great example of why scientific names are so important. Because more than one species has the common name rockweed, the scientific name lets scientists, and other seaweed enthusiasts, know exactly which species of seaweed is indicated.

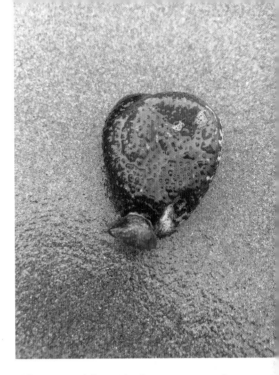

This seaweed from the brown seaweed group is called "studded sea balloon" (*Soranthera ulvoidea*) and is about the size of a loonie. It looks like a small, partially deflated balloon covered with bumps. It grows in the northern Pacific Ocean.

Phyco-fact
People have been using seaweed as a medicine for at least 3,500 years!

My daughter helping me harvest bull kelp in the kelp forest. *Agathe Bernard*

Red Seaweeds

The red seaweed group includes seaweeds such as nori, rainbow seaweed, dulse, Turkish towel, Turkish washcloth, Irish moss and coralline algae. Seaweeds in the red family can be shades of red, pink, purple or, like some types of nori, almost black.

Phyco-fact

There are about seven thousand species of red algae, also called **rhodophytes**, in the world.

Phyco-fact

Several Coast Salish First Nations harvest black nori, which is also called "black weed." They have been harvesting nori as a traditional food for many generations.

Opposite, top left to bottom right: Turkish washcloth, *Mastocarpus* spp.; Irish moss, *Chondrus crispus*; Dulse, *Palmaria* spp.; Coralline algae, *Corallina vancouveriensis* (*Emma Geiger*); Turkish towel, *Chondracanthus* spp.; rainbow seaweed, *Mazzaella splendens*.

Nori

Pyropia abbottiae

Porphyra umbilicalis

Nori is the most popular seaweed in the world. It is the seaweed used to make sushi, and it is sold in thin strips that are eaten as a snack. In Ireland it is known as *sleabhac*, and in Scotland and England it is known as *laver*. There are many kinds of nori, just like there are many kinds of apples. In the North Atlantic you can find *Porphyra umbilicalis*. *Pyropia abbottiae*, often called black nori, grows off the west coast of Canada and the United States as far south as Northern California, and is a traditional food of several Coast Salish First Nations. In Japan, South Korea and China, *Pyropia yezoensis* and *Pyropia tenera*, two other types of nori, are grown on farms in the ocean. Almost all the nori used in sushi and "seaweed snacks" comes from these farms!

Black nori grows on the shores of Vancouver Island, where I live, in the high intertidal zone where it's easy to collect without even getting your feet wet if you go to the beach when the tide is low. Even though black nori is in the red seaweed group, it looks black when wet and is see-through!

Nori has a rubbery texture that makes it difficult to cut with a knife, so when I harvest nori, I use scissors instead. I am *very* careful when I cut a piece of nori still attached to a rock because it is one of the easiest seaweeds to pull off its

Black nori, *Pyropia abbottiae*

rock. This is because it has a tiny holdfast. After I have cut a piece, I take it to the ocean and rinse it really well to get rid of sand and sometimes even sea creatures like isopods. Isopods have little hook-like claws on their feet that make them stick to the seaweed. When I gently pull an isopod off the nori, their little feet stick to me! Isopods will not hurt you, so if you see one, gently put it back on some seaweed that is still anchored to a rock.

Once you have some pieces of well-rinsed nori, you can dry them by spreading them onto cooling racks you would normally use for cookies and leaving them out on your counter for a day or so.

Isopods like this one love to hide in the frilly folds of seaweeds such as sea lettuce (pictured here) and nori. If you find one, be sure to carefully put it back on a piece of seaweed that will be staying in the ocean!

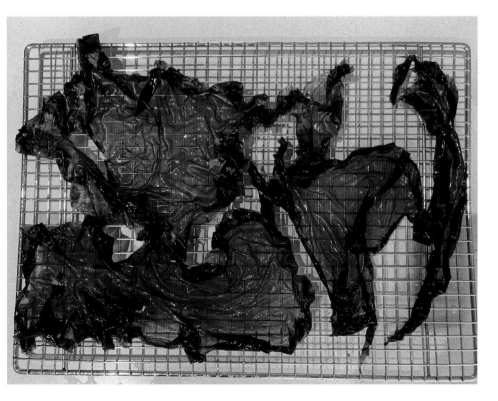

Nori spread on a cooling rack to dry.

Nori Crisps

Nori is a delicious seaweed. My favourite way to eat nori is to toast it in the oven until it is crispy.

Ingredients

- About 20 grams dried nori
- 1 Tbsp (15 mL) toasted sesame oil or olive oil

Directions

1. Toss dried nori in oil, trying to coat all the seaweed.
2. Put the seaweed on a cookie sheet in the oven at 170°F (75°C).
3. Cook for 6 minutes and then flip the seaweed using tongs.
4. Cook for 6 more minutes, or until crispy.
5. Eat right away or store in a glass jar with the lid on for one week (don't put it in the fridge).

Nori sheets can be used to make sushi, eaten as a snack or made into a hat! *Amy Matthews*

Protein Powerhouse!

Nori has more protein than any other edible seaweed. Some types of nori can be composed of fifty percent — or half — protein! Our bodies need protein to grow and stay healthy.

Christina Symons

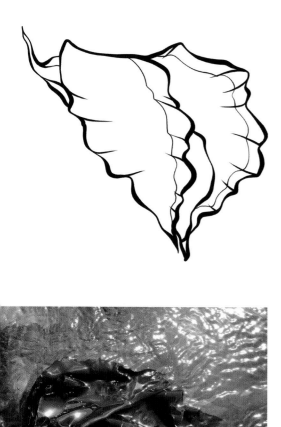

Rainbow Seaweed 🌀

Mazzaella splendens

Rainbow seaweed is one of the most beautiful seaweeds in the world. I call it "magical seaweed," because even though it is dark purple, if you see it in the water on a sunny day it shimmers all the colours of the rainbow. The first time you see it, you may think you have found a collection of beautiful, sparkling gemstones! Rainbow seaweed is iridescent, which means you can see different colours appear and disappear. I don't eat rainbow seaweed, but I bring it into the bath with me and rub it over my skin to make my skin feel soft. It can also help heal rashes and scrapes and relieve itchy skin. I don't usually cut rainbow seaweed, like I do with other seaweeds that I like to eat. Instead, I harvest it by salvaging (see page 30). When I find nice pieces of rainbow seaweed washed up on the beach, I take them home and dry them. Once they are dry, I put them in a resealable plastic bag or a glass jar and keep it beside my tub. If I am having a bath the same day I find a piece, I just throw it right into the tub without drying it!

Phyco-fact

The Hawaiian word for forgiveness, *kala*, is also the name of a Hawaiian seaweed. This seaweed is used in a traditional Hawaiian forgiveness and reconciliation ceremony called Hoʻoponopono.

Magical Rainbow Bath

1. Find a nice piece of rainbow seaweed that has washed up onto the beach.
2. Fill your bathtub with warm water.
3. Put your piece of rainbow seaweed into the tub.
4. Rub it on your skin to make your skin feel soft. Place gently on any cuts or scrapes or itchy areas for several minutes to help heal and soothe the skin and to prevent infection.
5. Feel the magic of the beautiful, shimmery seaweed that flashes different colours.

You can make a "seaweed hand bath" by putting rainbow seaweed (and others if you want) into a bowl with warm water. Place your hands in the bowl and rub the seaweed over them. This is a wonderful treat to give someone on their birthday or just as a spontaneous gift. It nourishes the skin and makes hands feel soft.

When rainbow seaweed is dry, it is plum purple and looks like normal seaweed. But when it is wet, it magically shimmers all the colours of the rainbow (see opposite page).

Red Seaweeds 93

Mermaid Yearning

I have always been enchanted by mermaids—how fiercely independent they are, their natural curiosity and how their best friends are always delightful sea creatures. And I love their long, flowing hair and the surreal, deeply beautiful sound of their singing. But the biggest reason I have always wanted to *be* a mermaid is because they can breathe underwater.

I want to be able to breathe underwater because all my favourite animals live beneath the surface of the ocean: dolphins, humpback whales, sperm whales, orcas, sting rays, manatees, sea turtles, lobsters, sea cucumbers and more. Magical creatures like sea horses live there too, and so do alien-like creatures such as jellyfish and octopuses. Several kilometres under the sea live such bizarre-looking fish it seems they were designed for a science-fiction movie. There are even mythological creatures that are said to live in the sea, like the kraken: a sea monster resembling an enormous octopus, which legend has it is capable of dragging huge ships down to the ocean abyss.

When I was little, I developed a technique for breathing underwater that I truly believed would work, and I used to practise it in the bathtub. While I never could breathe underwater, I got really good at holding my breath. When I had the chance to snorkel in the ocean, I would dive down to the bottom to see all the different creatures who lived there. From the surface, the bottom just looked like sand and rock or coral. But once I dove down, different types of creatures would appear. When I was thirteen, I got my SCUBA license. Finally, I could breathe underwater, but not for as long as a mermaid can. Just for as long as the air in the tank on my back lasts.

These days, I dive all the way to the bottom each time I am harvesting seaweed in the kelp forest. When the tide is high, I have to dive deeper to reach the bottom than when the tide is low. I don't kick my legs separately, like racing swimmers do, but I swish them up and down together, as if I have a mermaid's tail. On every dive to the bottom I see so many cool things, and each one feels like a gift. There is a mat of colourful seaweeds covering the bottom of the kelp forest, with well-disguised fish hiding there. Sometimes I see a big Dungeness crab

I love holding my breath and diving deep under the ocean. *Chris Adair*

moving stealthily through the flowing seaweed. If I'm lucky I might see a lingcod hanging just above the bottom, motionless, like a spooky statue, or a female kelp greenling, indigo blue and yellow and covered with orange spots, swimming slowly around the bull kelp stipes.

One time I was swimming along the bottom and my mask was just a few inches away from a dramatic-coloured rock greenling—purplish brown with fluorescent orange splotches—before I saw it. What a surprise! I sometimes see jellyfish like the beautiful sea nettle, with long, dusty-pink tentacles, or the star-shaped, fiery red lion's mane jelly, or the fried egg jelly, which looks just like a fried egg and has very long, clear tentacles. The bodies of jellyfish, called bells, pulse to an unearthly rhythm and their tentacles move about as if they have minds of their own. Jellyfish look as though they may have come here from another planet. Sometimes the large silver-grey back of a seal flashes into my view, and then just as quickly disappears into the dark, emerald-coloured depths.

After a long time in the kelp forest, I sometimes feel like I am still there even after I am on dry land. My body still feels the gentle rocking of the sea, and when I close my eyes, the glowing green hue of the water filled with bull kelps, their blades flowing in the current, is all I see. Sometimes, after I fall asleep, I am visited by whales in my dreams.

I have often wished I was a mermaid because I have a yearning to live under the sea. Have *you* ever dreamed of what it might be like to live under the sea?

Dulse

Palmaria mollis

Palmaria palmata

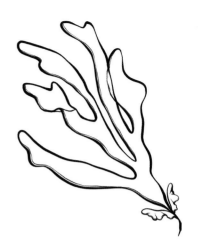

Dulse grows in the low intertidal and subtidal zones. People have harvested dulse in the Canadian provinces of Nova Scotia, New Brunswick and Prince Edward Island for several hundred years. It is a common snack food in those Atlantic provinces as well as in Maine, just south of the border in the US. Dulse is also a popular food in Ireland, where it is called *dillisk*. There, it has been used for centuries as a medicine to rid the body of parasites.

I harvest dulse in the spring when the tide is low, so it is exposed or in very shallow water. I use a knife to carefully cut some of the seaweed while leaving some of it attached. To dry dulse, you can hang pieces of it on a clothesline or in low tree branches. At night, you will need to take it inside to finish drying. Inside, you can hang it on a wooden clothes-drying rack or plastic hangers, or just lay your pieces on baking sheets. Make sure not to use metal hangers because the salty seaweed will make them rust. Once the pieces are dry, you can store them in a resealable plastic bag or a glass jar with a lid. You can also buy dulse at your local health-food store and in some grocery stores.

Pacific dulse, *Palmaria mollis*

Pacific dulse, *Palmaria mollis*

Atlantic dulse, *Palmaria palmata*

This seaweed from the red group looks like earthworms without the rings. It is called "rubber threads" (*Nemalion vermiculare*).

Mermaids' Mineral-Rich Snack

Ingredients

- Dulse, dried
- Roasted almonds, hazelnuts, pecans or your favourite nut

Directions

1. Cut or tear the dulse into bite-sized pieces.
2. Mix the dulse and nuts together in a bowl, or pack the mixture into a bag and bring it with you to the beach.

Christina Symons

Mighty Minerals!

Seaweeds have more minerals in them than any other food! Our bodies need minerals for almost everything we do. We have minerals in our blood and bones, and our brains need minerals to send messages to our bodies about important things like breathing and moving. Where do seaweeds get all these minerals? They absorb them from the seawater. That's right! Saltwater doesn't just contain salt. It contains lots of other minerals too.

Dulse spread out to dry on a screen in my seaweed shop.

Turkish Washcloth

Mastocarpus spp.

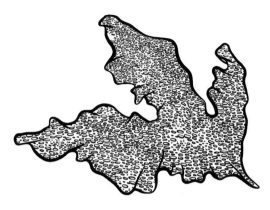

Turkish washcloth grows in the mid-intertidal zone and the high intertidal zone. The best thing to do with Turkish washcloth is to use it as a natural scrubby in the shower or bath. The reason it is a good scrubby is because it is covered with little bumps called **papillae**. If you are camping on the beach, you can use Turkish washcloth to scrub off your dirty dishes.

Christina Symons

Turkish washcloth doesn't always look like a seaweed. For part of its life, it looks like a dark crust growing on a rock. You can see this phase of the Turkish washcloth on the left of the photo and the larger phase on the right.

Phyco-fact

Seaweed and microalgae can be made into fuel for cars and airplanes! Fuel made from plants or seaweeds is called biofuel.

Medicine from the Sea

In Ireland, the name *carrageen moss* can refer to two different seaweeds: Irish moss (*Chondrus crispus*) and a seaweed that is in the same genus as Turkish washcloth, *Mastocarpus stellatus*. In cooking, both are used to thicken and set liquids, but they have also been used as medicine for hundreds of years. Irish people have used carrageen moss to help heal chest infections such as pneumonia and bronchitis, to expel phlegm and to prevent viral infections.

Make Seaweed Gel

This mermaid-approved gel can be used as a spa treatment, a thickener for food or a slippery slime-like substance to play with!

Ingredients

- About 1 cup (250 mL) Irish moss or Turkish washcloth, fresh or dried
- Water
- Optional: Juice of ¼ lemon

Directions

1. Put seaweed into a bowl, cover with tap water and let sit for 10 to 15 minutes.
2. Drain water, move seaweed to a large pot and add enough water to just cover the seaweed.
3. Bring to a boil, then remove from heat and let soak for 20 minutes.
4. Scoop out seaweed with a slotted spoon and place into a blender (add lemon juice, if using).
5. Add ¼ cup (60 mL) of water and blend on high speed until it becomes a creamy consistency.
6. Remove from blender using a spatula and place into a glass jar with a lid.
7. Store in the fridge for up to 2 weeks.

Christina Symons

Christina Symons

How to Use Your Seaweed Gel

1. Add 1 Tbsp (15 mL) to smoothies or oatmeal for added nutrition and a thick, creamy texture.
2. For a mermaid spa experience, rub onto skin. Relax while gel dries, then gently rinse off.
3. After shampooing, apply instead of a hair conditioner, then rinse to add softness and shine.
4. Seaweed Gel has a mild SPF (Sun Protection Factor) — the amount of UV protection depends on the type of seaweed used.

Turkish Towel

Chondracanthus spp.

Like Turkish washcloth, Turkish towel is covered with papillae, which makes it an excellent natural scrubby. Because it is larger than Turkish washcloth, it is called Turkish towel. It can be harder to find than Turkish washcloth because it grows in the low intertidal zone and subtidal zone, which means it is usually covered by water. If you are lucky, you will find fresh, beautiful pieces washed up on the beach after it is windy. You can use Turkish towel the same way you use Turkish washcloth.

Turkish towel is covered with bumps called papillae, which makes it an excellent scrubby.

Seaweed Bath Bomb

Christina Symons

Materials

- Glass jar with lid
- Mold for forming your bath bombs (you can buy a mold specifically for making bath bombs or you can use silicone muffin cups or measuring cups)
- 1 cup (250 mL) baking soda
- ½ cup (125 mL) Epsom salt
- ½ cup (125 mL) cornstarch
- 2 tsp (10 mL) dried, flaked seaweed (kelp, rockweed, Turkish towel, Turkish washcloth, Irish moss)
- 2 Tbsp (30 mL) coconut oil
- 5 to 7 drops of essential oil (I recommend eucalyptus, grand fir, mandarin or orange)
- ¾ Tbsp (11 mL) water
- ½ cup (125 mL) citric acid
- Optional: Treasure to hide inside your bath bomb such as a small pretty shell or ocean-themed trinket.

Directions

1. Mix together baking soda, Epsom salt, cornstarch and seaweed flakes in a large mixing bowl.
2. Warm coconut oil in a pot on low heat until it is a liquid.
3. Mix liquified coconut oil, essential oil and water in a glass jar with lid screwed on tightly and shake well.
4. Pour contents of jar into the mixing bowl with the dry ingredients, add citric acid and mix together well with

your fingers. The consistently should be like crumbly beach sand. A little fizzing is normal at this stage, but do not add water as that will cause your mixture to release all its fizz in the bowl, rather than in your bath.

5. Press mixture into your molds. Use the back of a large spoon to press mixture tightly into the molds.

6. Let dry in molds for at least 2 hours but not longer than overnight. Remove mixture from the molds, being careful not to break them because they are very fragile at this point, and put onto wax or parchment paper to dry (one to two days).

7. When your Seaweed Bath Bombs are completely dry, wrap them. You can use colourful cloth, tissue paper or pretty wrapping paper tied with a bow. Alternatively, you can store in a glass jar with a lid.

Enjoy Your Seaweed Bath Bomb

Draw a warm bath. Drop your Seaweed Bath Bomb in. Watch it fizz and enjoy the beautiful scents of the seaweed and the essential oil.

Christina Symons

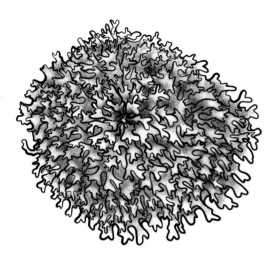

Irish Moss

Chondrus crispus

Irish moss grows in the Atlantic Ocean off the east coast of Canada and the northeastern United States, and on the west coast of Europe. In Ireland it has been used as a very important medicine to treat respiratory illnesses such as pneumonia, bronchitis, colds and sore throats. Irish moss can be eaten, and it is most often used to thicken liquids such as sauces and puddings. A substance called carrageenan is extracted from Irish moss as well as some other red seaweeds and used as a thickener in foods such as ice cream, salad dressings, soy milk, beer, sauces and processed meats. It is also used in some kinds of toothpaste, shampoo and skin creams.

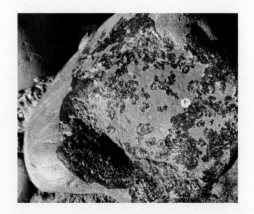

See that black stuff on the rock that looks like tar? It is actually a seaweed belonging to the red seaweed group. It is called tar spot. Its scientific name is *Ralfsia* spp.

Why Is a Seaweed in the Red Group Brown?

When we talk about seaweeds as being red, brown or green, we are referring to the biological group that they belong to. Although most red seaweeds are a shade of red, pink or purple, brown seaweeds are most often a golden brown, and green seaweeds are usually a shade of green, sometimes they are not. For seaweeds such as dead man's fingers, it is as if they didn't get the memo about what colour they are supposed to be!

Red eyelet silk (*Sparlingia pertusa*) is a beautiful, pinkish-purple seaweed with lots of little holes that grows in the Pacific Ocean.

Dead Man's Fingers

Halosaccion glandiforme

Dead man's fingers belongs to the red seaweed group, but it is actually greenish brown. The inside of this seaweed is filled with seawater and the outside has tiny holes, which makes it an excellent seaweed squirt gun! If you are looking for one to use as a squirter, make sure you only use dead man's fingers that you find unattached on the beach. If you rip up dead man's fingers that are attached to a rock, then they really will become dead!

Dead man's fingers growing with other seaweeds. *Emma Geiger*

Dead man's fingers squirt water in every direction when squeezed!

Nitrogen fertilizer is used on large industrial farms to grow food for both humans and animals and produces a gas called nitrous oxide, which depletes the ozone layer and contributes to global warming. Seaweed obtains all of its nutrients from seawater and doesn't require any fertilizer to grow. Eating seaweed is good for both you and the planet.

Better Burps for the Earth!

As part of the process of digesting their food, cows burp out a gas called methane, which is a greenhouse gas. Greenhouse gases cause the Earth to get warmer. Believe it or not, there are so many cows burping out methane that it is a major contributor to climate change. What does this have to do with seaweed, you might ask? Well, a red seaweed called *Asparagopsis taxiformis* can help. When just a small amount of this seaweed is added to a cow's food, it can reduce the amount of methane they burp out by more than 80 percent!

Asparagopsis taxiformis is a very prized seaweed in Hawaii. Its Hawaiian name is ʻkohu. *Nalani Kaneakua*

Coralline Algae

Coralline algae are a group of seaweeds belonging to the red seaweed group, and they are usually a pretty shade of pink. For a long time, scientists thought they were coral. They look and feel like coral, because they have **calcium carbonate** in their cell walls, which makes them hard like coral. Coralline algae can be found growing in every ocean in the world!

Coralline algae growing on a rock.

Seaweed Greeting Cards

Seaweed is beautiful, mysterious and fascinating, and it can make some spectacular art. Making seaweed greeting cards is one way to share this beauty with others. The first step in making a seaweed greeting card is to make seaweed pressings. Making seaweed pressings is like forming a giant sandwich. It takes about three days for seaweed pressings to dry completely. After they are dry, you can then assemble your seaweed greeting cards.

Part 1: Make the seaweed pressings "sandwich"

Materials

Christina Symons

- Shallow pan
- Your favourite fresh seaweeds (Delicate seaweeds work very well for this project, but avoid very thick seaweeds. If using dry seaweed, soak first.)
- Scissors
- 140-lb watercolour paper in sheets that are 21.6 cm × 28 cm (8.5 × 11 inches) or smaller (from an art supply store)
- Paintbrush, medium-sized
- 3 to 5 pieces of cardboard that are slightly larger than your watercolour paper
- Newspapers (or paper towels)
- 3 to 5 sheets of wax or parchment paper (depending on how many seaweed pressings you want to make)
- 3 or 4 heavy books
- Mod Podge (from an art supply store)

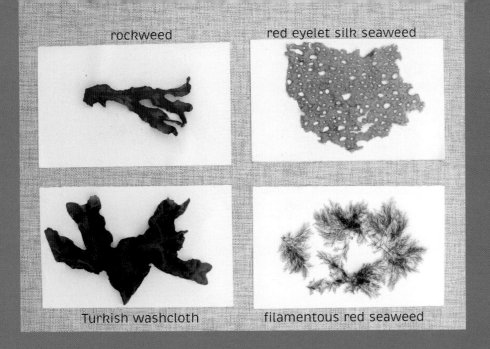

rockweed

red eyelet silk seaweed

Christina Symons

Turkish washcloth

filamentous red seaweed

Directions

1. Pour water into a shallow pan so the water is about 4 cm (1.5 inches) deep.

2. Put your seaweed into the water.

3. Cut a piece of watercolour paper in half and slide one half into the water and underneath the seaweed.

4. Holding the paper in one hand, use your paintbrush to spread the seaweed out onto the paper how you would like it to look.

5. Lift the paper slowly and gently until it is out of the water and the seaweed is lying on top of it. Put it to one side and repeat this process to make more than one seaweed greeting card.

6. Put your first piece of cardboard down with a couple pieces of newspaper on top of the cardboard. Put your first seaweed paper on top of the newspaper.

7. Very carefully lay a piece of wax or parchment paper on top of your seaweed paper, being careful not to move the seaweed.

8. Lay more newspaper on top of the wax or parchment paper, lay a piece of cardboard on top of that, and then some more newspaper.

9. Put your next seaweed paper on top of the newspaper and place wax or parchment paper, newspaper and cardboard on top.

10. Repeat until you have done this with all of your seaweed papers.

11. On top of last piece of cardboard, put several heavy books. The weight of the books helps press the seaweed onto the paper.

12. The next day, carefully open your "seaweed pressings sandwich" and change the newspapers and wax paper with fresh pieces. Do this once per day for the next three days. The reason we do this is so your pressings can dry and not get mouldy.

13. If your seaweed is completely dry after three days of switching the newspapers and wax paper, you can move on to the final step. If they aren't dry, continue changing the newspapers and wax paper once per day until they are.

14. Gently paint the top of the seaweed on your paper with Mod Podge. This protects your seaweed and helps secure it to the page so that your seaweed pressing lasts longer.

Part 2: Make your greeting cards

Materials

- 21.6 cm × 28 cm (8.5 × 11 inch) sheets of cardstock (from an art supply store), one for every card you want to make
- Multi-purpose white glue
- Seaweed pressing

Directions

1. Fold a piece of cardstock in half.
2. Spread glue over the back of one of your seaweed pressings.
3. Stick your seaweed pressing to the top side of your folded cardstock.
4. Wait for 1 hour and then your card is ready! Write a message on the inside and give to someone!

Christina Symons

Green Seaweeds

The green seaweed group includes seaweeds such as sea lettuce, green rope and sea staghorn. Seaweeds in the green family can be dark green, light green or a bright emerald green.

Phyco-fact

There are about six thousand species of green algae, also called **chlorophytes**, in the world.

Opposite, top left to bottom right: green rope, *Acrosiphonia* spp.; *Prasiola* spp.; sea lettuce, *Ulva* spp. (*Emma Geiger*); sea staghorn, *Codium fragile*; sea grapes, *Caulerpa* spp.

Sea lettuce with a baby kelp crab.

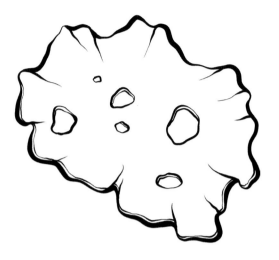

Sea Lettuce

Ulva spp.

Sea lettuce is a bright green seaweed that grows in all areas of the intertidal zone and also grows in the subtidal zone. It grows on many coastlines around the world. Little crabs, as well as isopods, sometimes use it as a place to hide. Sea lettuce is delicious! I love to eat it in salad, on popcorn, or just dried on its own as a snack.

Phyco-fact

Green sea turtles love to eat sea lettuce!

Sea lettuce with a sea star.

Sea Staghorn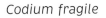

Codium fragile

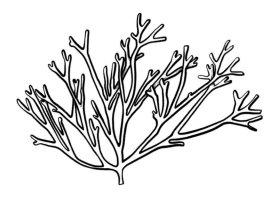

Sea staghorn is a green seaweed that grows in both the North Atlantic Ocean and the North Pacific Ocean. It is squishy, like a sponge, and in some places it was used to make a tea to rid the body of parasites.

Sea staghorn has the common name "dead man's fingers" in some regions. Be sure not to confuse it with the red seaweed that shares this common name, listed on page 110. The scientific name for the red seaweed known as "dead man's fingers" is *Halosaccion glandiforme*.

Mermaid Salad

Ingredients

For the salad:

- Fresh greens
- Sea lettuce, cut into bite-sized pieces
- Pumpkin seeds (their fun green colour matches the other greens)

For the dressing:

- 1 Tbsp (15 mL) olive oil
- 1 tsp (5 mL) lemon juice
- 1 tsp (5 mL) tamari
- 1 tsp (5 mL) tahini

Directions

1. Put salad greens and sea lettuce into a salad bowl (a wooden bowl is nice if you have one).
2. In a separate smaller bowl, mix together dressing ingredients. Stir vigorously until well blended.
3. Pour dressing over greens and sea lettuce.
4. Toss well with salad tongs.
5. Sprinkle pumpkin seeds on top.
6. Now your Mermaid Salad is ready to eat!

Christina Symons

Sea Grapes

Caulerpa spp.

Sea grapes is a green seaweed. In some places, it is eaten fresh and raw and is compared to the taste and texture of caviar (fish eggs). Sea grapes can grow in many parts of the world, including the Caribbean Sea, which is where I found the piece in the photo (opposite page). Each individual "grape" is made up of a single cell. These cells are among the largest known cells on Earth!

Phyco-fact

The giant sea anemone gets its beautiful blue-green colour from microalgae that live inside of it. Some sea lettuce is growing around this giant sea anemone.

Green Rope

Acrosiphonia spp.

This green seaweed looks like fine green hair. It can be found on both Pacific coastlines and Atlantic coastlines growing in the mid-intertidal and low intertidal zones.

Giant Pacific Chiton

Sharing the intertidal and subtidal zones with seaweed in the Pacific Northwest is the giant Pacific chiton, the largest species of chiton in the world. A chiton is a mollusk, which are often called shellfish. Other mollusks include mussels, clams, oysters, scallops, limpets and abalone. Giant Pacific chitons, sometimes called "gumboot chitons," eat seaweed. They aren't picky and will eat seaweed from all three groups: the browns, reds and greens.

Exploring the Kelp Forest

The Most Magical Place on Earth

The kelp forest is my favourite place in the whole world. It is eerie and magical and teeming with life. In the kelp forest, I have had seals tug on my fins, watched jellyfish as long as me pulsating in the current, and come face to face with a giant Pacific octopus. I have seen huge schools of fish, made up of thousands of individuals, swim as though they are a single creature, weaving around the stipes of the bull kelp.

Kelp forest ecosystems grow on temperate coastlines (a temperate coastline is one where the temperature of the water is cool) around the world. Some species of kelp do not float and just lie along the bottom of the ocean, while some species of kelp have either floats or rigid stipes that allow them to grow upward toward the surface. A kelp forest ecosystem requires upward-growing kelp, because this creates structure that forms a habitat for an abundance of different species. In the Pacific Northwest, there are three main seaweeds that form the structure of kelp forests, two of which

Opposite: This is me, diving deep beneath the canopy of the kelp forest to see the creatures that call the kelp forest their home.
Chris Adair

Bull kelp forest. *Chris Adair*

grow tall enough to reach the surface: giant kelp, the largest seaweed in the world, and bull kelp, the second-largest seaweed in the world. Walking kelp, the third main species, doesn't reach the surface.

I invite you to join me in the cold, emerald-green waters of the Pacific Northwest, underneath the canopy of the bull kelp, to meet the creatures who call the kelp forest their home.

At the Bottom

There are lots of different seaweeds that grow in a kelp forest. Covering the bottom of a kelp forest you will find kelp such as winged kelp, triple-rib kelp and five-rib kelp, and red seaweeds such as coralline algae.

There are also a *lot* of sea creatures that live at the bottom of the kelp forest, including limpets, abalone, chitons and sea urchins, which eat kelp. There are Dungeness crabs, red rock crabs, skates (they look like a stingray but they don't have a stinger) and fish that hide in the sand at the bottom, such as flounders, soles and sanddabs.

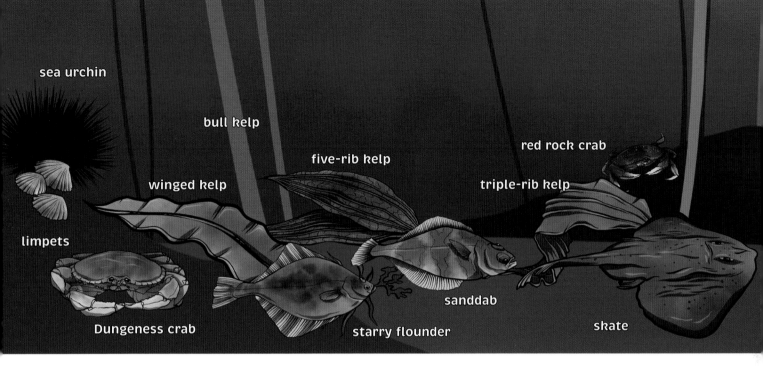

sea urchin

bull kelp

five-rib kelp

winged kelp

red rock crab

triple-rib kelp

limpets

Dungeness crab

sanddab

starry flounder

skate

Seaweeds and animals that live on the bottom in a kelp forest.

Flatfish on the Floor

Flounders, soles and sanddabs are called flatfish because instead of swimming upright like a regular fish, they swim on their side so they can blend in with the ocean floor. To help them live life swimming on their side, one of their eyes moves over and joins the other one on the same side of their head when they are very young! Flatfish usually have great camouflage and look exactly like the ocean floor.

This flatfish is called a rock sole. *Eiko Jones*

Limpets look like little pointy hats.

Phyco-fact

Kelp forest ecosystems are incredibly biodiverse. This means that they contain many different types of living things.

Parts of walking kelp (*Pterygophora californica*): holdfast (like roots), stipe (like a stem) and blades or fronds (like leaves).

Emma Geiger

Going Up!

A little higher up in the kelp forest, yet still attached to the bottom, you will find walking kelp. Walking kelp is the oldest seaweed that grows in the kelp forest, and it has a rigid, woody stipe that enables it to stand upright. Walking kelp are the old growth of the kelp forests, the way western red cedar, Douglas fir and Sitka spruce trees form the old growth in the temperate rainforest of the Pacific Northwest. Just like trees, you can count the rings inside their stipe to determine how old they are (on a tree, you count the rings inside the trunk). The stipe of walking kelp looks and feels like wood, but it is more bendy.

stipe

blades or fronds

holdfast

Some creatures like to hide under the walking kelp in a kelp forest, close to the bottom. This is where you will find fish such as lingcod, greenlings and rockfish. These kinds of fish stay near the bottom of the ocean and are called **bottom fish**. Greenlings can be very bright and beautiful colours!

Halfway Up

Above the tops of the walking kelp, but still underneath the canopy created by the blades of the bull kelp, you will find other kinds of sea creatures. There are jellyfish such as lion's mane jellyfish and fried egg jellyfish. There are fish

Walking kelp in a kelp forest. *Eiko Jones*

Rock greenling near the bottom of a kelp forest. *Eiko Jones*

Phyco-fact

Walking kelp can live to be twenty-five years old! That is very old for a seaweed.

bull kelp

sea lion

fried egg jellyfish

lion's mane jellyfish

orca

school of surf smelt

sea perch

salmon

Animals that live about halfway between the bottom of a kelp forest and the surface.

Phyco-fact

Sea otters sometimes wrap giant kelp or bull kelp around themselves so they don't float away while they are sleeping.

such as sea perch, salmon and sometimes huge schools of thousands of sand lance and surf smelt. Sometimes there are marine mammals such as sea lions, seals and even orcas!

Under the Canopy

High up in the kelp forest, and just beneath the canopy created by the blades of the bull kelp, you will find even more types of interesting sea creatures. Fish called tubenose poachers live here, as well as cross jellyfish and moon jellyfish. In the kelp forest in the summer, grey whales and

Fish Schools

Some fish form schools. In a school, fish move together, which makes them look like a single creature if you see them from far away. They can turn sharply, this way or that, in unison. Sometimes, when I am swimming through the kelp forest, there are so many fish that I can spin in a full circle and thousands of fish are all I can see.

Mighty Kelp

Remember, kelp are large seaweeds belonging to the brown seaweed group. The largest seaweeds on Earth are kelp. There are many different kinds of kelp that grow in kelp forests in the Pacific Northwest. In kelp forests in other parts of the world, there may be only a few kinds of kelp.

Here I am with a huge school of fish called sand lance. *Chris Adair*

Animals that live just beneath the canopy in a kelp forest.

humpback whales feed on tiny prawn-like animals called krill and on small fish.

Creatures That Live on the Bull Kelp

You can find kelp crabs, clingfish and tiny shellfish called *Lacuna* spp. living right on bull kelp in a kelp forest.

Kelp crabs are one of the most common creatures I see living on bull kelp. Even though kelp crabs can't swim, they can travel between the very bottom and the very top of a kelp forest. They do this by walking up and down the stipes of bull kelp. They evolved legs perfectly designed for

A fried egg jellyfish looks just like a fried egg!

Eiko Jones

kelp-stipe walking! Fish and marine mammals such as seals, sea lions, dolphins, porpoises and orcas can also travel quickly between the top and bottom of a kelp forest by swimming.

On Top of the Kelp Forest Canopy

The top of the kelp forest is like an island. The canopy of a bull kelp forest is created when the tops of the bull kelp stipes and the blades of the bull kelp are pulled together at the surface of the water by the ocean currents. This makes it

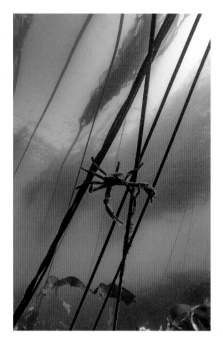

A kelp crab on bull kelp stipes. Sometimes I find kelp crabs on the blades of bull kelp that I am harvesting. When that happens, I carefully move them to the blades of a different bull kelp. *Chris Adair*

This is the egg sac of *Lacuna* sp. It looks like a tiny white donut. This one is attached to rainbow seaweed. A mature *Lacuna* sp. is shown on the opposite page.

Northern clingfish have little fins that are like suction cups that they use to stick onto blades of kelp.

darker underneath the canopy, because it blocks out a lot of the sunlight from above. The big bulb at the end of a bull kelp's stipe, which is filled with gases, is what makes the bull kelp float. Sometimes birds such as great blue herons, seagulls and cormorants land on top of the canopy and fish in the kelp forest below.

The Ecology of Kelp Forest Ecosystems

The **ecology** of a kelp forest ecosystem is the relationship between kelp and its environment. Kelp provide habitat, or

Lacuna spp. are tiny shellfish that are only about as big as ants. They love to eat seaweed!

A great blue heron stands on the canopy of a bull kelp forest scanning the water for fish.

Jack Chapman / Biosphoto

Exploring the Kelp Forest   **139**

a home, for many sea creatures. Kelp also provide food for sea creatures. Everything that exists inside a kelp forest is part of a kelp forest ecosystem. A kelp forest contains both living and non-living things that affect the ecosystem.

Some important non-living things, called **abiotic factors**, that affect kelp forests are water currents, water temperature, substrate (what the bottom is made of), salinity (how salty the water is), storms and pollution. In order for kelp to grow and be healthy, there need to be strong water currents, the water needs to be cold and salty, and the substrate needs

This wolf eel is eating a sea urchin. It must have tough lips to not get poked by the sea urchin's sharp spines! A wolf eel isn't actually an eel, but a fish. However, it looks like an eel because of its long skinny tail.

Bruno Guenard / Biosphoto

A very cute sea otter playing in bull kelp. Sea otters can eat a *lot* of sea urchins.

Jeremy Koreski

A sunflower star on top of winged kelp. Sunflower stars are the largest species of sea star in the world! Unlike most other sea stars, which have five arms, sunflower stars have many arms.

to be rocky. Severe storms can rip the kelp up and pollution can affect its ability to grow and reproduce.

Living things, or **biotic factors**, also affect the growth of kelp. Animals like sea urchins, limpets and abalone graze on kelp and, in turn, predators like sea otters, wolf eels and sunflower stars prey on them. Human harvesting of kelp is also a biotic factor that can affect the health of the kelp forest ecosystem. That is why it is important to always harvest sustainably and never rip seaweeds off of rocks.

A kelp forest ecosystem. *Chris Adair*

This area used to be a kelp forest, but lots of sea urchins ate all the kelp and now it is an urchin barren. Look how many sea urchins there are! *Scott Groth*

The Balance of Kelp Forest Ecosystems

Sea urchins *love* to eat kelp, including the holdfast that anchors kelp to the bottom. Sea otters, wolf eels and sunflower stars love to eat sea urchins. If there are too many sea urchins in a kelp forest and no predators to eat them, they can eat the whole kelp forest! When this happens, we call the large area that used to be a kelp forest—but which is now just bare rocks—an **urchin barren**. If there are sea otters, wolf eels or sunflower stars who live in the kelp forest and they eat some of the sea urchins, then there aren't enough sea urchins to eat the whole forest and they just eat some of the kelp. The presence of these predators in a kelp forest helps to create balance in the kelp forest ecosystem. When there is balance in the ecosystem, animals get enough to eat and the kelp remains healthy.

Mermaid Musings

Dreaming in Black and White

Ever since I began harvesting bull kelp in kelp forests that are several hundred metres out to sea, I have dreamed of coming face-to-face with an orca. When I am in the kelp forest, I often imagine seeing an orca through my mask, its huge black-and-white body filling my entire field of vision before curving to weave among the bull kelp stipes, which stand as pillars in the glowing green water. The thought of it is thrilling.

The southwest coast of Vancouver Island, where I live, is home to two distinct populations of orcas. One population is known as the **Southern Resident Killer Whales**, who eat almost exclusively salmon and are critically endangered, with only seventy-five individuals left. Every orca in this population is known and has been named by scientists who study whales. The other population of orcas are known as **transients**. Transient orcas eat marine mammals, most often seals and sea lions. It is not uncommon to see orcas in the waters near my home in the spring and summer months, and there is no feeling that compares to seeing their long, black dorsal fins carving through the green water against a backdrop of snow-topped mountains.

Although orcas are considered to be the top predator in the ocean—even great white sharks won't mess with

them—they have never been known to harm a human being in the wild. In fact, they are in the same biological family as dolphins, beloved for their friendly and curious nature.

The closest I came to having my dream fulfilled was on a hot summer day in late July while harvesting bull kelp. I woke up that morning to the sun shining and a chorus of birds singing outside my bedroom. After coffee and breakfast, I went out to my seaweed shop, which is where I hang the fresh, wet seaweed to dry, and began getting ready to harvest bull kelp. First, I pulled on my thick wetsuit, complete with booties, gloves and a hood. Even though the air temperature was very warm, the water where I live hardly changes temperature from the winter to the summer. It is always cold—about the temperature of the water that comes out of your cold-water tap—which is a good thing because kelp need cold water to grow and to be healthy.

After my wetsuit was on, I put my mask, snorkel and harvest knife in one of my harvest bags, a heavy-duty mesh bag with shoulder straps like a backpack, then loaded that, my other harvest bag and my long fins into my wheelbarrow. Finally, I loaded my wheelbarrow into my car and drove the one-minute trip to the beach that I can see from my home. When I arrived at the beach, I made my way down the trail to the water's edge. Once there, I pulled on my fins, fastened my harvest knife around my wrist with an elastic band which it is tied to, put on my harvest bag, picked up my mask and snorkel and prepared to enter a whole other world.

I made my way toward the water, walking gingerly down the beach with my long fins, and once I arrived, I turned around and entered the ocean backwards. If you have ever tried walking into the water with fins on, it is nearly impossible to do it walking forwards. I was quite hot by this point—in my thick wetsuit out in the summer sun—and the shock of the cold water came as a relief at first. In about waist-deep water, I turned around to face away from the shore, rinsed and then pulled on my mask and snorkel and slid the rest of my body into the ocean. The icy cold water on my face, the only part of me not covered by my wetsuit, was biting at first but soon faded to a familiar numbness.

I pushed my long fins up and down and watched the bottom of the ocean drift by. Ripples of sand gave way to stretches of sea lettuce and dulse until finally, bull kelps started to appear out of the whitish glow of sun rays hitting the emerald-green water. Bull kelp always reminds me of a gathering of mermaids: the long, narrow stipe their body, the round, hollow float their head and the blades their long hair flowing behind them in the ocean current. I took a moment to admire their beauty before I started to harvest.

I found a bull kelp that had long, beautiful blades. I took half the blades together in one hand and with my other hand I cut them, leaving about a half an arm's length still attached to the stipe so that the blades would continue to grow. It was as if I was giving the mermaids a haircut! With my face in the water, carefully examining what I was doing through my mask, I began the difficult task of getting all the blades, which were trying to float away in the current, into my harvest bag. When the last one was inside, I pulled the drawstring closed, keeping my precious bull kelp blades safely inside. Once I had harvested blades from a few more bull kelps, I let my harvest bag float on its own and prepared to do one of my favourite things in the whole world: hold my breath and dive under the canopy of the kelp forest. I took

a big breath in, held it, bent my body at the waist and then kicked hard to get myself deep under the water. It takes a lot of effort to dive under the water when you are wearing a thick wetsuit because neoprene, which is what wetsuits are made from, is very buoyant. Once I had made it under the water, I quickly saw a kelp greenling hanging motionless near the bottom and a small school of striped sea perch swimming slowly around the bull kelp stipes. I twisted on my side, swimming sideways like a flatfish and moving my legs together as if they were a mermaid's tail.

When my chest started to feel tight and my brain increased the urgency of the message that I needed air, I pried my eyes away from the spectacular underwater scene, looked up toward the surface and pushed my fins through the water, sending me upward. As I broke the surface and breathed a generous amount of air into my lungs, I spotted something. Farther out to sea, I could make out the shapes of about seven to ten orcas, swimming very fast, their black-and-white bodies leaping out of the water and then diving head-first back under. Such a rush of pure joy and excitement raced through my body that it felt like there were buzzing bees flowing through my bloodstream. My dream came true in that moment. I watched with reverence the fascinating display of these giant black-and-white dolphins, leaping and diving against the clear blue sky.

In spite of that treasured experience, I still dream with nervous anticipation of coming face-to-face with a magnificent orca in the kelp forest.

Chris Adair

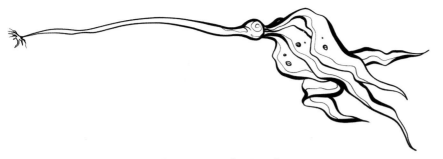

Sea you later!

We have reached the end of our seaweed journey together. I hope you have had fun learning some new and amazing things about seaweed and that the next time you see some at the beach, your curiosity will be ignited. I also hope that there is a special place in your heart, like there is in mine, for seaweed.

Happy seaweed exploring, from the Mermaid of the Pacific. See you at the beach!

Glossary

My seaweed apprentice, Josianne, and me in my seaweed shop with drying *Alaria* (winged kelp).

abiotic factors: Non-living things that affect an ecosystem

algae (singular alga): A diverse group of photosynthetic organisms that includes both microalgae and macroalgae (seaweeds)

biodiverse: Containing many different types of living things

biotic factors: Living things that affect an ecosystem

blade: A flat, leaf-like frond of a seaweed

bottom fish: Fish that live near the bottom of the ocean

calcium carbonate: A naturally occurring substance that is located in some living things such as coral and red algae

camouflage: The ability of an animal to look like its surroundings

carbon dioxide: A colourless and odourless gas that is released when we exhale, used by plants and seaweeds for photosynthesis and released into the atmosphere by the burning of fossil fuels

chlorophytes: A term used by phycologists that refers to green algae (seaweeds)

diatoms: A group of microalgae that have silica located in their cell walls

ebbing tide: A tidal current that is going out, which exposes more of a shoreline to air

ecology: The relationship between living things and their environment

flatfish: A flattened fish that swims on its side and has both eyes on the upper-facing side

float: An air-filled bladder which helps a seaweed float; also called a pneumatocyst

flooding tide: A tidal current that is coming in, covering more of the shore with water

food chain: The sequence by which food travels from organism to organism in an ecosystem

frond: The leaf-like part of a seaweed

fucoidan: A substance contained in brown seaweeds that is beneficial for human health

fucoxanthin: A substance contained in brown seaweeds that is used for photosynthesis and is beneficial for human health

genus: A rank used in the biological classification of living organisms; the first word of a two-word scientific name

giant Pacific octopus (*Enteroctopus dofleini*): A species of octopus that lives in the North Pacific; the largest species of octopus in the world

habitat: The natural environment where an organism lives

high intertidal zone: An area of the intertidal zone that is the farthest away from the water and is often exposed to air

holdfast: The part of a seaweed that anchors it to a substrate, such as a rock

Kelp crab on a bull kelp stipe. *Chris Adair*

intertidal zone: The area at the edge of an ocean or sea that is sometimes exposed to air due to tidal action

kelp: Large brown seaweeds that belong to the order Laminariales

kelp forest: A high density area of upward-growing kelp

low intertidal zone: An area of the intertidal zone that is usually underwater and is only exposed to air at very low tides

macroalgae: The formal word for *seaweeds*; also includes multi-cellular, freshwater algae

marine mammals: Mammals that live either their entire life or most of their life at sea (includes dolphins, whales, seals, sea lions and others)

microalgae: A group of microscopic, photosynthetic organisms

mid-intertidal zone: An area of the intertidal zone that is underwater about half the time and exposed to air about half the time

midrib: A thick, raised structure that runs linearly along the centre of a seaweed blade

minerals: Chemical elements, many of which humans need in very small amounts in order to be healthy

nutrient: A substance that provides nourishment essential for growth and the maintenance of life

oxygen: A colourless, odourless gas that is essential to the survival of almost every living organism

Pacific Northwest: A region of the west coast of North America that includes Alaska, British Columbia, Washington, Oregon and Northern California

papillae: Small outgrowths (bumps) that occur on some seaweeds and plants

perennial: A seaweed or plant that lives for more than two years

phaeophytes: A term used by phycologists that refers to brown algae (seaweeds)

photosynthesis: The process by which plants and seaweeds use energy from the sun to create nutrients in the form of sugars, which they use to grow; the process requires the absorption of carbon dioxide and water and releases oxygen

phycologist: A biologist who studies algae (which includes seaweeds)

phycology: The study of algae (includes seaweeds)

pneumatocyst: An air-filled bladder that makes a seaweed float; also called a float

primary producer: An organism that photosynthesizes

rhodophytes: A term used by phycologists that refers to red algae (seaweeds)

Salish Sea: An area of the Pacific Ocean that cradles the southern tip of Vancouver Island and includes the Strait of Georgia, Puget Sound and the Juan de Fuca Strait

salvaging: Collecting seaweed that has been ripped up by waves or wind

Beware the sea cabbage (*Saccharina sessilis*) monster!

scientific name: A two-word name biologists give to an organism; the first word is the name of the genus and the second word is the name of the species

seaweed: An informal term that refers to marine macroalgae

sedentary: Unable to move around

sodium alginate: A substance contained in brown seaweeds that helps to safely remove toxins from the body and is used as a thickener in foods such as ice cream, yoghurt and cheese

Southern Resident Killer Whales (SRKW): A population of orcas that live in the Pacific Northwest, who eat exclusively fish, primarily salmon, and are endangered

species: A group of similar organisms that are able to reproduce and produce fertile offspring

spore: A reproductive cell that can develop into a new individual

spore patch: A conspicuous patch that contains spores, which appears on some species of seaweed such as bull kelp

sporophylls: Modified parts of the seaweed frond that are reproductive

stipe: The stem-like part of a seaweed

subtidal zone: An area of the ocean that is always covered in water and is never exposed to air due to tidal action

sulphuric acid: A chemical that is a strong, corrosive acid

sustainable: Living in a way that is in balance with the environment

symbiotic relationship: Organisms of different species living together in a close relationship

transient orcas: A population of orcas that live in the Pacific Northwest and eat marine mammals, primarily seals and sea lions

urchin barren: An area of the sea floor where lots of sea urchins have eaten away all the kelp, leaving behind bare rocks

vitamins: Nutrients that are required by the body in order to grow and be healthy

zooxanthellae: A group of microalgae that live in a symbiotic relationship with invertebrate animals such as coral

Acknowledgements

I am very grateful and wish to say thank you to the following people who supported me in creating this beautiful book:

- Thank you to all the young students I have taught, whose enthusiasm about seaweed is such a pleasure to witness and helped inspire me to write this book.

- Bill and Sue Swinimer: Thank you for nurturing my innate passion for the ocean from a young age.

- Thank you to Jen Swinimer Silvester for your generosity: for brainstorming ideas with me, for your expertise editing the first draft of the manuscript, and for your supportive enthusiasm.

- Dan and Elaina Swinimer: Thank you for making me laugh out loud while we brainstormed ideas for the book's title.

- Sarah Harvey: Thank you for your help editing and developing the manuscript and for encouraging me to add "snappiness."

- Claire Watson: Thank you for your beautiful, fun and detailed illustrations.

- Chris Adair, Jennifer Jellett, Emma Geiger, Jeremy Koreski, Agathe Bernard, Kate Woods, Maxwel Hohn, Eiko Jones, Tien Bui, Christine Young, Thomas Frankovich, Nicole Yamamoto and Scott Groth: Thank you so much for contributing your beautiful photos. They add so much beauty and wonder to the book!

- My family and friends for being seaweed models: Mahina, Nesika, Maddie, Eva, Kirra, August, Mira, Faizal, Josianne, Alaria, Sunny, Maya, Tien, Kanahawele, Grayson, Vanessa and Violet.
- Caroline Skelton: Thank you for your skilful copyedit.
- Thank you to Libris Simas Ferraz for the beautiful book design.
- A special thank you to Anna Comfort O'Keeffe and Harbour Publishing for believing in the value of seaweed education and providing the expertise and support to produce this beautiful book.

These photos are of my two biggest fans and were taken in my seaweed shop when I first became a professional seaweed harvester back in 2003. On the left is my dad with *Alaria* (winged kelp) hanging to dry and on the right is my mom, peeking through the drying bull kelp.

References and Recommended Reading

Druehl, L., & Clarkston, B. (2016). *Pacific Seaweeds: A Guide to Common Seaweeds of the West Coast*. (Updated and expanded ed.). Harbour Publishing.

Lamb, A., & Hanby, B. P. (2005). *Marine Life of the Pacific Northwest: A Photographic Encyclopedia of Invertebrates, Seaweeds and Selected Fishes*. Harbour Publishing.

Rhatigan, P. (2009). *Irish Seaweed Kitchen: The Comprehensive Guide to Healthy Everyday Cooking with Seaweeds*. Booklink.

Sept, D. J. (2008). *A Photographic Guide to Seashore Life in the North Atlantic: Canada to Cape Cod*. Princeton University Press.

Swinimer, A. (2021). *The Science and Spirit of Seaweed: Discovering Food, Medicine and Purpose in the Kelp Forests of the Pacific Northwest*. Harbour Publishing.

Watling, L., Fegley, J., & Moring, J. (2003). *Life Between the Tides: Marine Plants and Animals of the Northeast*. Tilbury House Publishers.

Index

sausage seaweed. *See* soda straws
    seaweed
scientific naming, 46, 85
sea cauliflower (*Leathesia*
    marina), 58
sea grape (*Caulerpa* spp.), 124–25
sea lettuce (*Ulva* spp.), 9, 89, 120
sea otter, 65, 134, 141–42
sea staghorn (*Codium fragile*), 121
Seaweed Bath Bomb, 106–7
Seaweed Gel, 103-4
Seaweed Greeting Cards, 114–17
sieve kelp (*Agarum clathratum*),
    5, 76
soda straws seaweed
    (*Scytosiphon* sp.), 66
sodium alginate, 21
southern resident killer whales, 143
spore patch, 47–48
spores, 54
sporophylls, 54–55
stipe, 7, 8, 132
storage of seaweed, 36
stringy acid weed, 29
studded sea balloon (*Soranthera*
    ulvoidea), 85

sugar kelp (*Saccharina latissimi*), 76
subtidal zone, 12–13
sun protection, 82, 84
sustainability. *See* harvesting

tar spot (*Ralfsia* spp.), 108
tea as medicine, 124
Tea of Land and Sea, 73
tidal zones, 12–13
tide times, 26
transient orcas, 143
Turkish towel
    (*Chondracanthus* spp.), 24,
    86, 105
Turkish washcloth
    (*Mastocarpus* spp.), 86,
    101–2, 115

urchin, 76, 130, 135, 140–42
urchin barren, 135, 142

walking kelp, 130, 132–33
winged kelp (*Alaria marginata*), 26,
    35, 43, 46, 53–55
wolf eel, 140, 142

About the Author

Jennifer Jellett

Amanda Swinimer (BSc Marine Biology) lives on the west coast of Vancouver Island, BC, with her two daughters. She is the author of *The Science and Spirit of Seaweed: Discovering Food, Medicine and Purpose in the Kelp Forests of the Pacific Northwest* and has her own business, Dakini Tidal Wilds, hand-harvesting wild seaweed from the beaches and kelp forests surrounding her home. Swinimer's unique expertise makes her a sought-after speaker at international conferences about the ecological and environmental importance of seaweeds. She has been conducting seaweed tours and workshops and teaching young people in the British Columbia school system for two decades, passing on knowledge about the health benefits of seaweeds and sharing her intensely joyful connection to the ocean with diverse audiences. Her first love is her responsibly harvested seaweed, which is sold to some of British Columbia's finest restaurants and is available through her website.